The Cover Quiz

The cover of this document includes the photos of many of the Canadians included in this e-book who are listed as mentors or who received mentoring.

If you can identify the names of all of the people in the photos in any vertical, horizontal, or diagonal row, you will be eligible to receive any e-book published by Peer Resources at no cost or become a member of the Peer Resources Network at no cost (a $99.00 value).

To view the e-books published by Peer Resources or review the benefits of membership in the Peer Resources Network, visit this link.

Once you have identified the people in the photos, send an email to rcarr@mentors.ca

A sample quiz with the photos of Canadian mentors and the answers are displayed in the box to the right.

Top Row:
Nancy Southern Alan Thicke Bruce Cockburn Celine Dion

Second Row:
John Horgan Elizabeth May Rona Ambrose Ron Southern

Third Row:
Carole James Justin Trudeau Irwin Cotler Margaret Laurence

Bottom Row:
Mark Messier Lisa Raitt, neema, David Cronenberg

Shaping the Future: 150+ Canadian Mentoring Relationships That Make Canada Great, Creative, Innovative, Productive, Successful and Welcoming

A Celebration of Canada's 150th Birthday

Rey A. Carr
Peer Resources
Victoria, British Columbia

June, 2017

Created, designed and produced in Canada.

Copies of this e-book are available at no-cost from online sources.
Details are available at http://www.peer.ca/mentors.html

Peer Resources
1052 Davie Street
Victoria, British Columbia V8S 4E3
Canada
Tel: (250) 480-9698
Email: info@peer.ca
Twitter: @Peer_Resources

Library and Archives Canada Cataloguing in Publication

Carr, Rey A., author
     Shaping the future : 150+ Canadian mentoring relationships that make Canada great, creative, innovative, productive, successful and welcoming : a celebration of Canada's 150th birthday / Rey A. Carr, Peer Resources.

Includes bibliographical references and index.
ISBN 978-1-895890-53-2 (PDF)

     1. Mentoring--Canada. I. Title.

BF637.M45C37 2017   658.3'124   C2017-903797-8

Dedication

I am grateful to have had so many mentors in my life. Some mentors provided shoulders to stand on that allowed me to see the world more clearly:

John Seward
Mike Sanson
Mervin Freedman
Nevitt Sanford
Pierre Trudeau

Some mentors extended hands that guided me in worthwhile directions:

Dwayne Hawk
Vincent Price
John F. Kennedy
Tom Gordon

Some mentors offered their hearts to help me through difficult passages:

Vance Peavy
David de Rosenroll
Arthur Kratzmann
The Harvest Moon Group (you know who you are)

Some mentors shared their wisdom to guide me to my True North:

Leo Buscaglia
Wayne Dyer
Marianne Williamson

I appreciate all you've done for me and I pledge to continue to pay forward an unlimited amount of mentoring to others.

TABLE OF CONTENTS

Additional Online Resources about Mentoring

The following links to information, documents and resources are based on those most requested by visitors to Peer Resources' website, and the most frequently asked questions regarding mentoring. The entirety of the website is non-commercial and advertising-free. The home page for the website features information not only on mentoring, but also on peer assistance and coaching.

Peer Resources relies on one-time member fees to support its not-for-profit activities.

- Tips on Finding and Working with a Mentor (Link to Peer Resources' website)
- Want to Be A Great Mentor? (Link to Peer Resources' website)
- The Complete Database of Mentoring Pairs (Link to Peer Resources' website)
- The Best Mentoring Experts and Consultants (Link to Peer Resources' website)
- The Best Mentoring Options for Youth In Canada: Big Brothers Big Sisters Canada and Boys and Girls Clubs Canada
- The Top CEO/Executive Fee-Based Mentoring Groups (Link to Peer Resources' website)
- The Best Books and Videos on Mentoring (Link to Peer Resources' website)
- The "Who Mentored Whom" Quiz (Link to You Tube)
- The Steps Associated with a Peer Mentoring Group for Seniors (Free article download)
- Notable Quotes Used for Mentor Training Workshops (Free E-book download)
- Become a Member of the Peer Resources Mentoring, Coaching and Peer Support Network (Link to Peer Resources' Products Bookstore)

Wondering If You Are a Mentor or If You've Had a Mentor in Your Life?

Many people are uncertain as to whether they have had a mentor or whether someone else considers them a mentor. This is not unusual. There are many stereotypes or myths about mentoring that reduce the likelihood that people will recognize mentoring in their own lives. To counteract this and help people identify mentors in their life or acknowledge their own role as a mentor, we created the Mentor Quiz, which consists of 15 questions that can be answered "Yes" or "No." Try the Mentor Quiz here and see your status in mentoring.

Introduction

Mentoring has been a large and increasing part of Canadian culture. Both formal and informal mentoring are present in virtually every aspect of Canadian life, including the workplace, schools, colleges, universities, community settings, and social support groups.

The purpose of this white paper from Peer Resources is to celebrate mentoring by estimating how Canada ranks compared to the U.S.A. as a place for mentoring; provide details about what is involved in mentoring; describe the foundations of mentoring and how it differs from coaching, supervision, and training; examine cultural differences associated with mentoring; and most importantly, illustrate a sample of the variety of Canadian mentoring relationships from all areas of life that are included in the Peer Resources Mentor Hall of Fame.

150 Years of Mentoring in Canada

Canada may be the world's leader when it comes to mentoring relationships. While specific data on the number of mentoring connections that exist in Canada and other countries is sparse, data does exist on volunteerism, which is the basis for most mentoring relationships.

According to data released in 2013 by Volunteer Canada, 60% of Canadians volunteer, 44% of which engage in formal volunteer activities, and 82% of which volunteer in informal activities. Compare this to the United States where the volunteer rate is less than 25% (a rate that has been falling slowly since 2011. (https://www.bls.gov/news.release/volun.nr0.htm)

Why do so many Canadians volunteer? According to Volunteer Canada, the six main reasons Canadians like to volunteer are to contribute to the community, use their skills and experience, network or meet people, improve a sense of well-being or health, explore strengths, and sign up because a friend had done so. The main motivation for volunteering in the USA is to provide service for a religious organization

In 2001 Peer Resources created the mentoring strategy for Canada's National Stay-in-School Initiative (2001-2004). They recruited 30,000 volunteer mentors from communities and businesses across Canada and paired them with 100,000 students at risk of dropping out of school. Since that pioneering project, literally hundreds of organizations have been established in Canada to pair mentors with those who desire mentoring. (For a list of those organizations, visit the Peer Resources' Find a Mentor page.

Youth Mentoring in Canada

<u>Boys & Girls Clubs of Canada</u> estimates they had over 15,000 volunteers in 2016 to provide help to Canadian youth—not all were mentors.

<u>Big Brothers Big Sisters Canada</u> has mobilized 21,300 volunteers in 2016 to mentor 41,700+ children and young people—a total of 2.2 million volunteer hours for the year.

<u>Futurpreneur Canada</u> is a national, non-profit organization that provides financing, mentoring and support to business owners aged 18-39. Their mentoring program facilitated 1100 matches between mentors and entrepreneurs in fiscal year 2016/2017.

collecting, preparing, distributing, or serving food. Tutoring or teaching account for about 9% of volunteer activity in the USA. In almost every area of life, such as social services, religion, sports and recreation, Canadians provide a higher percentage of volunteers than the USA.

Canadians tend to agree on what barriers they experience to providing volunteer help. Sixty-five percent say lack of time; 61% don't want a long-term commitment; 56% prefer to donate; and 51% say they don't volunteer because "no one asked." Not surprising, beliefs about mentoring based on reasons 1 and 2 (it takes a lot of time and requires an infinite commitment) have been addressed in the <u>literature</u>, and persons who have been involved in successful mentoring relationships discount those two reasons.

What is Mentoring?

While the professional and popular literature is fairly consistent about a definition of mentoring, for the purposes of these mentoring relationships, we conclude that there are two kinds of mentoring: FORMAL AND INFORMAL.

Formal mentoring relationships have the following characteristics:

- a deliberate, conscious, voluntary relationship:
- they may or may not have a specific time limit;
- they are sanctioned or supported by the corporation, organization, or association (by time, acknowledgement of supervisors or administrators, or are in alignment with the mission or vision of the organization);
- they occur between an experienced, employed, or retired person (the mentor) and one or more other persons (the partners);
- they typically take place between members of a school, college, business or civic organization, corporation, or association, or between members of such entities and individuals external to or temporarily associated with such entities;
- the mentor and partner are generally not in a direct, hierarchical or supervisory chain-of-command;
- the outcome of the relationship is expected to benefit all parties in the relationship (albeit at different times) for personal growth, career development,

lifestyle enhancement, spiritual fulfillment, goal achievement, and other areas mutually designated by the mentor and partner;
- the relationship may also benefit the community or organization within which the mentoring takes place;
- the mentoring activities take place on a one-to-one, small group, or by electronic or telecommunication means; and
- the mentoring relationship is typically focused on interpersonal support, guidance, mutual exchange, sharing of wisdom, coaching, and role modelling.

Informal mentoring relationships have the following characteristics
- they can include many of the characteristics of a formal relationship;
- they are often reciprocal, where the mentor and the partner learn from each other;
- they are often managed from a distance and may include the mentor and partner never meeting in-person;
- they typically are characterized by what the partner learns from the mentor;
- they are typically life-long relationships; and
- informal mentoring is often carried out without the mentor knowing what impact he or she has had on the partner.

How Does Mentoring Differ from Other Helpful Roles?

Over the years Peer Resources has received hundreds of enquiries about the differences between mentoring and coaching (as well as therapy, consultation and supervision). Having engaged in all five roles (actually six, if I include the role of client, partner, consultee or supervisee), I can attest to the value of clarification. Role clarity decreases boundary problems, sharpens focus, and pinpoints expectations. Such clarity also leads to a deeper sense of purpose and commitment. But highlighting differences can lead to missing the similarities. All five areas, for example, represent ways to help people learn, change, and manage adversity. All five require a relationship of trust, understanding, and authenticity. And all five base their success on the ability to listen.

In 1999 I prepared a chart that lists differences between coaching, mentoring and therapy based on ten criteria, and I held the naive view that this would be the definitive list (Carr, 1999). Other experts believe the differences are simpler as in the distinction that Margo Murray (2001), a leading expert in mentoring, stated by saying that "mentoring is a process and coaching is a verb." Some contributors to the Peer Resources' Twitter feed support this view: "Coaching is a skill good mentors use and mentoring is a process," according to one contributor.

> *"If a mentoring relationship does not make the both the mentor and partner better persons, then it's probably not mentoring"*
>
> ~ Rey Carr ~
> Peer mentoring pioneer
> Mentored by John Seward

The most popular distinction made by our Twitter contributors is the voluntary nature of mentoring as compared to the fee-based aspect of coaching and therapy. One would-be Twitter poet chimed: "When it's free, I can be me; when I pay, show me the way."

Other contributors recognized the importance of relationship in both coaching and mentoring, but distinguished the two by saying that mentoring was more personal and coaching was more impersonal. While most agreed that a mentor is seldom responsible for the resulting actions of the partner, there was less agreement about the degree to which the coach is responsible for the client's success. The mentor may point a person in a certain direction and provide support, but takes no responsibility for the outcome.

Coaching is seen as a more professional relationship where the coach may believe he or she has some responsibility to help the client make the necessary changes. For example, one contributor wrote: "A coach helps somebody do what they already know is the right thing to do. A mentor helps a person to determine the right thing to do." Another web visitor said: "Mentoring gives a personal touch. It's like the advice of a best friend, but coaching is just for the sake of the job."

Not everyone is worried about these distinctions, and many practitioners are content to leave such details to academics. A website contributor summarized this viewpoint by saying, "In the future, making distinctions between terms such as these two (coaching and mentoring) will prove futile and unproductive. Fewer people will be interested in definitions and roles and more people will be interested in results and practicalities."

A recent enquiry about the differences between mentoring and coaching, as well as a question presented to a LinkedIn discussion group on this same topic, led us to conduct a search on Google. To our surprise and amazement the search produced more than three million hits. Three million different takes? (Maybe there were only 10 credible links and the remaining millions were phishing schemes based on the popularity of mentoring and coaching?)

Without repeating in entirety what we have been emphasizing over the years about the differences, the gist of our response is that there are far more similarities between the two ways of helping others than there are differences. We've also said that the search for the definitive answer to the question is unproductive and may even lead to considerable misinformation based on stereotypes and lack of experience.

Blurring the Boundaries of Mentoring

Recently the imaginary line that separates mentoring and coaching has become less precise as coaches, for example, more frequently offer what they call "mentor coach" services, and business entrepreneurs in a variety of niche areas offer mentoring for a fee, thus eliminating what used to be one of main distinctions between the two areas: one is paid (coach) and the other is a volunteer (mentor).

The International Coach Federation (ICF) recently provided an "approved definition of ICF mentor coaching" stating that mentor coaching is "coaching on coaching-competency development of the applicant-coach as opposed to coaching for personal development or coaching for business development, although those aspects may happen very incidentally in the coaching for competency development" (Marum, 2011). In most coaching communities and organizations in Europe this role would be considered supervision, not mentoring. Not coincidentally the way a person qualifies to be an ICF- approved mentor coach typically involves paying a fee for such a service.

> *"You can't start a fire without a spark."*
>
> ~ Bruce Springsteen ~
> American musician
> Mentored by Pete Seeger
>
> (From our companion ebook, "Mentoring Quotes")

In addition, I recently attended a mentoring conference where a well-known expert gave a keynote that was advertised as being about mentoring, during which one of the international mentoring experts at my table turned to me and said, "Isn't the speaker referring to coaching and not mentoring?"

Some of the published documents purporting to distinguish between mentoring, coaching and therapy often use models of each that seem outdated, stereotyped, uninformed or exaggerated just to strengthen their own perspective. To make matters more confusing, a few well-known coaching sources have chimed in on the answer to this question, and, surprisingly, have in many cases actually reversed the characteristics associated with each.

Mentor and Miracle Are Not the Same

The coaching industry is not the only area forging new ground or transcending the boundaries associated with traditional mentoring. Michael Garringer, Director of

Knowledge Management for Mentor: The National Mentoring Partnership , noted that the effectiveness of formal mentoring with some youth populations has led to the application of mentoring with "higher-risk youth" such as children of incarcerated parents, gang-involved youth, homeless youth, youth who have suffered abuse and trauma, teenagers in juvenile detention, children and adolescents with disabilities, and most recently, youth who have been victims of sex trafficking. In some cases the expectation is that mentors would be able to bring about behavioural changes usually associated with the intervention of therapists, supervisors, probation officers, case workers, teachers, and child care workers.

Similar high expectations have been expressed by adult visitors to our website who complete our Find a Mentor form. Many of the requests for mentors are accompanied by goals that typically include a desire for immediate results. In many cases we refer the Find a Mentor applicants to coaching services such as The Coach Connection or individual coaches who are members of the Peer Resources Network in order to help them sort out their goals, increase their own creativity in their search for results, make the changes they want to make, and achieve the results they desire.

The Four Pillars of Informal Mentoring

Many of the confusions associated with the distinctions between mentoring and coaching have arisen because more and more mentor leaders adopt and transfer the principles associated with informal mentoring. Informal mentoring has been such a powerful and memorable way of being with another person that it seems like a "slam dunk" to apply these principles to formal mentoring schemes. This transfer from informal to formal has been made to appear easier as experts have attempted to distill the elements associated with successful informal mentoring and adapted, adjusted or just plain "plunked them down" on formal mentoring program requirements.

> *"There is confusion about mentoring and coaching skills. Part of the challenge is the terms are used interchangeably. Explaining the difference between mentoring and coaching with definitions and examples can help managers change their style...Employees will have questions and need practical information and examples on how to mentor and coach."*
>
> ~ Valerie Pelan ~
> President of Integrated Focus
>
> (From our companion ebook, "Mentoring Quotes")

In many cases this transfer has been highly successful, yet there are certain elements that contribute to the effectiveness of informal mentoring that are yet to be fully captured by formal mentoring schemes. They can occur, and leaders of formal mentoring programs may do their best to facilitate them, but they are often more subject to factors beyond the control of the program design.

The details of the Four Pillars that follow, and the examples about particular outcomes that I believe are primarily associated with mentoring, are not exclusive to mentoring; and I'm sure that many, if not all, my coaching colleagues would hope that their work as coaches would result in similar outcomes.

As an introduction to the real life examples following the end of the Four Pillars section, I will identify the four elements that I believe distinguish mentoring from coaching. These four characteristics are derived primarily from my personal and professional experience as a mentor and as a recipient of mentoring, and they reflect an evolution of my learning since I proposed the original list of 10 distinctions back in 1999.

Pillar I: Mentoring is About Lessons for Life

Simply put, I believe that mentoring has to do with learning something that you might not have learned on your own or possibly might have taken you much longer to learn on your own. While some mentoring connections are initiated today to achieve short-term performance or behaviour changes (or there is an expectation that such changes will be the primary outcome), the historical and predominant element associated with mentoring is the influence it has on spiritual growth and development. I'm not referring to

> *"The benefit of spiritual partnership is authentic power. Authentic power is the life that your heart longs to live—fulfilled, grateful, caring, patient, fully present, meaningful, creative, and loving. When you realize these things about spiritual partnership, the most important question you can think of, the question that most urgently requires an answer, the question that you have been asking all your life becomes, How do I create spiritual partnerships? How do I become authentically empowered? How do I support others in creating authentic power?"*
>
> ~ Gary Zukav ~
> American best-selling author, former Green Beret, and award-winning science writer
>
> (From our companion ebook, "Mentoring Quotes")

religion here, but instead to higher consciousness, character values, and a way of being in the world.

I'm also not referring to gaining specific life skills or accomplishing tasks as soon as possible. Instead, I'm referring to spiritual input that enables a person to discover, practice, and master his or her own way of integrating the mentor's lesson into action (Zukav, 2010). And there may be times when such action might take place years after the contact with the mentor has been completed or ended. It's almost as if the life lesson lies dormant in consciousness until a particular circumstance or opportunity appears.

This delayed response is why so many people can vividly recall certain individuals from their past and recite almost word for word a particularly influential dialogue. A common thread associated with this delayed response is that most people did not recognize or call the person a 'mentor' at the time of the actual interaction. Yet, years may have gone by before they realize they were, at the time, in the presence of a mentor that had an influence on their spiritual being.

Pillar II: Mentoring is About Relationships

The essence of any mentoring relationship is the relationship itself. It is the relationship that determines whether anything of value is transferred between the mentor and the partner. Whether the mentor acts as a teacher, guide, catalyst, role model or any of the other dozen roles that have been enumerated, the key factor as to whether there is a transmission of knowledge or wisdom depends on the quality of the relationship.

And while the quality of the relationship may need time to develop, there are innumerable examples where such a relationship develops instantly. In addition, there are many times when the mentoring relationship can occur without ever having physically met or had a conversation with the other person. This is why so many people can have a mentoring impact, that is, provide lessons for others that last a lifetime, without actually knowing each other.

Certainly, factors such as trust, rapport, and caring (and a sense of humour) are important in any helping relationship, particularly to ensure effectiveness in today's formal mentoring programs, but such factors are not relevant in many informal mentoring relationships because the quality of the mentoring connection is based on a spiritual relationship. I'm not referring to a cognitive or intellectual connection, but instead to something beyond cognition, often something that is beyond memory, and resides more in a higher level of consciousness—a spiritual memory.

Pillar III: Mentoring is About Paying It Forward

Almost every person who has been involved in an effective mentoring relationship perceives mentoring as a gift, and they often demonstrate their appreciation and gratitude by passing on some aspect of their mentoring experience to others. Whether it is the life lesson, a particular piece of wisdom, a way of being, or the desire to act as a mentor to others, the gift is more often than not passed on to others.

This experience of paying it forward, and particularly the willingness to act as a mentor to others, is one of the most powerful reasons that mentoring has continued to grow exponentially throughout society. Canadian William Gray, founder and president of Corporate Mentoring Solutions, a British Columbia-based international mentoring consulting firm, was among the first to recognize that the "The proteges of today are the mentors of tomorrow."

While the following anecdote about the gift of mentoring and paying it forward may be unusual, it demonstrates the unexpected outcomes and influence of mentoring.

A high school math teacher in Seattle, Washington was gathering his materials at the end of the school day as he prepared to leave for home. Appearing at his classroom door was a former student who had since become one of the most highly successful dot-com entrepreneurs in the computer software industry. They both recognized each other immediately, and embraced while expressing great appreciation for seeing each other again.

The dot-com entrepreneur stated that he recalled during his days in that high school math class that his mentor had talked about how much he wanted to have a real sports car, but couldn't really afford one on his teacher's salary. The former student handed his mentor a set of keys and said, "Look out the window."

> *"One of the most potent of the weapons of influence around us is the rule of reciprocation. The rule says that we should try to repay, in kind, what another person has provided us."*
>
> ~ Robert Cialdini ~
> Social psychologist
>
> (From our companion ebook, "Mentoring Quotes")

There, sitting in the parking lot, was a brand new Porsche sports car with a ribbon on top. "Your encouragement and unwillingness to give up on me had such a powerful impact on my life that I wanted to find a way to make your dreams come true as well. I hope you like it," said the entrepreneur to his mentor.

The mentor was stunned. The generosity and thoughtfulness of the gift was extraordinary, but he also was stunned to learn that the impact of his mentoring, which seemed so much a part of his way of being, had played such a significant role in the life of his former student.

Then, he remembered that back in the days when the entrepreneur was a student in his class the math teacher had also talked about how he and his wife wanted to have a baby. He looked at his former student and said, "Should I be calling my wife and finding out what you've left at my house?"

The pay it forward pillar is also one of the primary reasons that more formal mentoring programs have been initiated in so many communities around the world. Initially fueled by successful adults recalling an individual from the past that had a significant positive impact on their life direction and choices, these formal programs have been initiated to re-create or provide similar experiences for children, teens and young adults. Whether these formal programs will act as a catalyst for participants who will be just as eager to pay it forward is not clear at this time.

> *"A real friend and mentor is not on your payroll."*
>
> ~ Prince ~
> Inducted into the Rock and Roll Hall of Fame in 2004
> Mentor to Carmen Electra
>
> (From our companion ebook, "Mentoring Quotes")

Pillar IV: Mentoring is About Mutuality

Most effective mentoring relationships grow and develop in a way that maximizes the exchange of value between both parties. Typically, the relationship begins with the mentor taking the lead and the partner responding to the mentor's questions or comments. Sometimes as the relationship develops it is characterized by a relatively equal exchange of questions and comments; and, as it grows further, an effective mentoring relationship evolves with the partner taking the lead and acting as a mentor to his or her mentor. Eventually, an observer would be unable to determine which person was the partner and which person was the mentor.

This mutual exchange is neither unique to or exclusive to mentoring. Such exchanges are often at the core of other forms of helping such as Re-evaluation Co-Counseling, Peer Mentoring Groups, mutual aid or self-help groups, Mutual Aid Counselling (developed by one of my mentors R. Vance Peavy) and various training activities where practitioners take turns acting in the practitioner and client roles.

This pillar of mutuality is also commonly found to exist in many kinds of relationships and has been called The Law of Reciprocity which has been described by many authors including my favourite, Robert Cialdini (1993). It is also known as the Golden Rule of "Do unto others as you would have others do unto you."

Illustrations of the Four Pillars

Background

I attended a school that was designated by the school board as an experimental high school. This fact was not known by me, my parents or the 3000 other students that represented the multi-ethnic diversity of our city. We all thought that the programs and activities at the school were part of a normal high school and what we were experiencing occurred at the nine other public high schools in the city.

One of these experimental programs was their peer mentoring service which identified every incoming student and assigned each one to an upperclass student (known as 'Eagles' after the school's mascot) to provide orientation, support, and guidance.

The Eagle assigned to me, Dwayne, an athlete but with a 'ducktail' and a-shirt with rolled up sleeves, came to my house during the summer to introduce himself. My mom told him I was at the park across the street playing first base for my junior high in a baseball game against a rival school. He came to the field to meet me and watch me play.

After the game, as my teammates and I were gathering our equipment and getting ready to go buy candy, gum and sodas, Dwayne came up to me, stuck his hand out to shake hands, and said, "Hi Rey, I'm Dwayne and when you come to Washington High I'm going to be helping you find your way."

That handshake foretold what would become one of the most significant relationships in my life.

Discussions With Dwayne Over Our Two Years Together	Life Lessons Learned as a Result
Don't judge people by how they look or what they wear.	Seek to understand
If you like someone and want them to like you, find out what she's interested in.	You learn more by listening than talking
Think for yourself. Don't let others tell you what to do.	Trust your feelings as well as your brain
Your actions and reactions determine your reputation.	What you do for others is who you are
You can't predict how much a curve ball will drop.	No matter what adversity you face in life, do your best

Illustrations of the Four Pillars

Background

During my mediocre career as a baseball player for my university team, I had a particularly bad day on the field. At the end of the game, our coach had the habit of gathering the team together to do what he called "debriefing." His approach consisted mainly of singling out certain players and peppering them with comments about how bad they played. None of the team members looked forward to or appreciated this style of "coaching."

He would occasionally ask an open-ended question like "What were you thinking?" but he never waited for an answer, so it was less a question and more of a condemnation. On this day we played and lost to our traditional rivals, consistently rated as the number one team in the NCAA.

When the team meeting was over, I put my glove and spikes in my bag and started across the field for the place I was living which was just a few hundred yards from the field.

As I was walking, I felt a presence come up behind me and was surprised to see my introductory psych teacher, Dr. John Seward catching up to me.

He put his hand on my shoulder and said, "Looks like you had a tough day on the field." All of a sudden a gush of tears came forth and I started sobbing while at the same time trying to say something comprehensible in response.

I said, "You watched the game?" And his reply stunned me. He said, "I did; and I came purposely to see you play 'cause you were in my class."

I was even more speechless since I was one of several hundred students in that class. He asked me to come and see him in his office the next day so we could talk about what happened to me on the field.

I came to his office feeling some trepidation and intimidation since I'd never met one-on-one with a professor before, and I thought I'd get kicked out of class. Instead, he offered to listen while I shared how my dream career was no longer a reality. His support became a foundation for my future success.

Discussions With Dr. Seward Over Our 3 Years Together	Life Lessons Learned
Don't be afraid of being afraid. Consider it a prompt telling you something essential about life.	Learn from your fears
When bad things happen or when life presents obstacles to your passion & dreams, examine what it means and decipher the message.	Let adversity be a teacher
The pursuit of perfection is fruitless, but the mistakes you make on the way can provide clues as to what to do next.	Learn from mistakes
Curiosity and imagination are the foundations of scientific enquiry.	Open your mind, particularly when you think you know it all
Working as a teaching assistant in this class is not about grading papers but helping students do their best.	Your purpose in life is to strive to bring out the best in yourself by bringing out the best in others

Illustrations of the Four Pillars

How Vincent Price Became a Mentor

I had a part-time delivery job during university working for a famous Beverly Hills/Hollywood drug store that served the movie and entertainment industry. One of the best and most surprising mentoring relationships came when I delivered one of many future orders to the home of the great star of horror movies Vincent Price.

He actually asked me questions about my life and when he found out I was taking an art history class, he invited me into his home which was filled with original works of classic art as well as paintings of his own. He took me on a tour, asked me questions about what I saw, and shared anecdotes about the artists. He encouraged me to take wild guesses, make jokes, and be creative. I said, "I guess from your movies, you actually knew some of these artists from the Renaissance."

How Jack Kennedy Became a Mentor

In 1960 I eagerly volunteered to work in the Los Angeles office to elect John F. Kennedy the 35th President of the United States. He would be the first presidential candidate I would be old enough to vote for, and I was honoured to work on his campaign.

During the election campaign he visited the LA headquarters, shook hands with every person in the office, and remarkably had something to say or ask of each person; and even more remarkable, he listened to every answer or answered any question. The electricity I felt when he took my hand in his and looked me in the eye, saying my name, thanking me for my service, and asking what I was studying at university, was all I needed to follow him anywhere and count him as a mentor for the rest of my life.

How Leo Buscaglia Became a Mentor

A friend worked as a teaching assistant to Dr. Leo Buscaglia, known as "Dr. Hugs" or the "The Love Doctor." She invited me to attend one of his classes and stay and meet him. After class she introduced me and he embraced me with a bear-like hug. Leo took both of us by surprise because when he let go of the hug, he stood back and said, "So what's keeping you two from being with each other?" Even though I was enrolled at a different university I showed up to each of his classes after that.

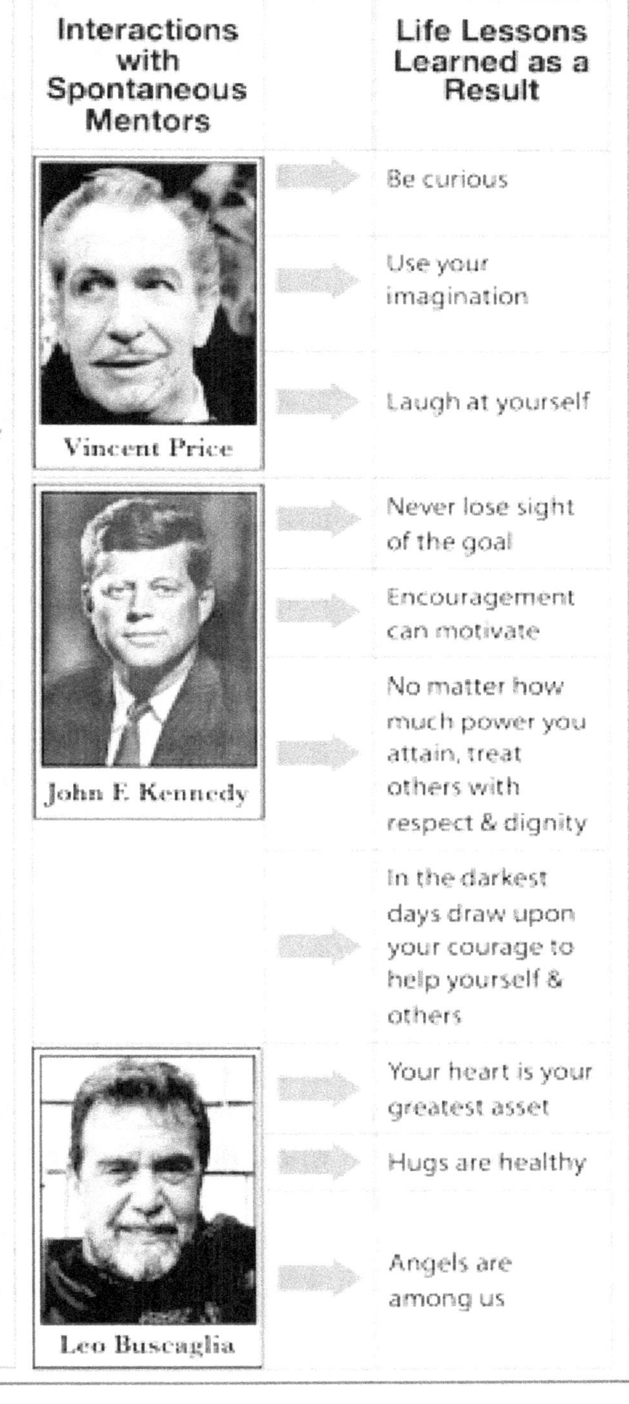

Interactions with Spontaneous Mentors	Life Lessons Learned as a Result
Vincent Price	Be curious
	Use your imagination
	Laugh at yourself
John F. Kennedy	Never lose sight of the goal
	Encouragement can motivate
	No matter how much power you attain, treat others with respect & dignity
	In the darkest days draw upon your courage to help yourself & others
Leo Buscaglia	Your heart is your greatest asset
	Hugs are healthy
	Angels are among us

Unique Language Associated with Mentoring

For the last 15 years, I have been curating a list of mentor pairs from a variety of sources including autobiographies, biographies, newspaper articles, personal interviews, and diligent historical research.

The pairings are divided into ten categories. (1) Actors, Comedians, Producers and Directors (Stage, Screen and TV); (2) Mentoring relationships depicted in motion pictures and television; (3) Musicians, Songwriters, and Singers; (4) Classical and Broadway Musicians, Composers, Conductors, Ballet, and Modern Dancers; (5) Fashion, Media and Celebrities; (6) Artists, Writers, Photographers, Publishers, Novelists, Poets; (7) Mentoring relationships depicted in print (novels stories, fiction); (8) Sports Figures, Athletes, and Coaches; (9) Historical, Political, Spiritual and Civic Leaders; and (10) Business, Industry, Education, Science, and Medical Leaders.

In many cases, the mentoring relationship is one between a mentor who has died and a person who they mentored who is still living. When I first started detailing this type of relationship, I referred to the relationship in the past tense: 'the person who died **was** a mentor to the person who is still living.' For example, when referring to the mentoring relationship between Canadian professional ice hockey player and scout Garnet "Ace" Bailey (1948-2001), who perished in World Trade Center air crash and Canadian superstar professional ice hockey player and team owner Wayne Gretzky, one could say that "Ace" was a mentor to "The Great One".

But that description using the past tense would be totally wrong with regards to mentoring. That is one of the aspects of mentoring that makes it different from virtually all other types of relationships. A true mentor helps you learn something better or faster, and that learning lasts your entire life. In other words, what you learn from a mentor does not disappear, fade, or stop when the mentor perishes. What you learn from a true mentor stays with you all your life; it's not temporary, it's a permanent part of you as a person (Carr, 2017).

Therefore, when a mentor dies, we don't say he or she "was" a mentor to so and so. Instead, we say, the person who died "is" a

> *"Mentoring is a system that uses the power of relationship to accelerate learning; whereas coaching is a system that examines where one wants to go, where one is, and how to close that gap."*
>
> ~ Rey Carr ~
> CEO, Peer Resources
> Mentor to Wayne Townsend, Canadian teacher, author, and founder of Peermentor.net
>
> (From our companion ebook, "Mentoring Quotes")

mentor to so and so. And if the mentor is a true mentor, the mentoring influence remains regardless of what has happened to the mentor. In some cases, for example, people might refer to someone as a "former" mentor or a person is "no longer a mentor." A true mentor is a mentor for life even when there is no longer an active relationship. This is one of the outstanding qualities of mentoring; one that distinguishes mentoring from coaching, training, and supervision.

When both persons in the mentoring relationship have died, then it is appropriate to refer to the relationship was in the past tense. For example, Canadian social democratic politician **Major** (his name not his military rank) **James Coldwell** (1888-1974) "was" a mentor to Canadian politician and founder of North America's first single-payer, universal health care program **Tommy Douglas** (1904-1986).

The Source of These Mentor Listings

This list of mentor pairs was compiled by <u>Rey Carr</u> from autobiographies, biographies, newspaper articles, obituaries, personal interviews, and diligent historical research. The criteria for inclusion required either person in the pair to be referred to as a "mentor" (or "protege") by the other person in the pair or by a third party knowledgeable about the relationship between the pair. In addition, to be included in this e-book one or both of the persons must be a Canadian.

The mentoring pairs listed here have been selected from as larger mentoring pairs database (referred to by Peer Resources as "<u>The Mentor Hall of Fame.</u>") There are likely thousands more mentoring pairs in Canada than are mentioned here. In some cases, mentoring was inferred because of details regarding life-long lessons learned from the "mentor."

Not all mentoring relationships require a face-to-face or personal connection. It is possible to perceive another person in the "spirit of mentoring;" that is, life lessons are learned from the person at a distance, possibly through reading or studying the life of another. Some of the mentoring connections listed here qualify as mentoring spirit relationships.

Some listings may appear in more than one of the categories listed because of multiple career activities or cross-career relationships.

If you know of other mentoring pairs that ought to be included or you find data that appears inaccurate, please email: <u>rcarr@mentors.ca</u>.

150+ Canadian Mentor Pairings to Celebrate Mentoring and Canada's 150th Birthday

Mentors Involved in Politics, History, Civic or Spiritual Leadership

- American academic, president of Harvard University and cousin of Nobel Prize-winning poet T.S. Eliot, **Charles William Eliot** (1834-1926) was a mentor to Canada's 10th Prime Minister **William Lyon Mackenzie King** (1874-1950), who in 1997 was rated by a group of Canadian scholars in *Maclean's* magazine as the finest of all Canada's prime ministers.

- Overcoming the adversity of his youth and becoming an advocate for those struggling for their rights, Saskatchewan-born Canadian aboriginal and community leader and recipient of Order of Métis Nation, **Jim Sinclair** (1933-2012), President of the Congress of Aboriginal Peoples of Saskatchewan, was a mentor to Assembly of Manitoba Chiefs Grand Chief **Derek Nepinak,** a member of the Minegoziibe Anishinabe (Pine Creek First Nation).

- Champlain, Quebec-born union leader and politician **Jean Marchand** (1918-1988), known as "one of the three wise men", was a mentor to Montreal, Quebec-born law professor and author **Pierre Elliott Trudeau** (1919-2000), 15th Prime Minister of Canada.

- Winnipeg, Manitoba-born **Mitchell Sharp** (1911-2004), a Canadian politician and Companion of the Order of Canada, is a mentor to Shawinigan, Quebec-born politician and statesman **Jean Chrétien,** the 20th Prime Minister of Canada.

- **John Chrétien,** the 20th Prime Minister of Canada, is a mentor to Stephenville, Newfoundland-born businessman and former Premier of Newfoundland **Brian Tobin;** Revelstoke, British Columbia-born lawyer and politician **John Nunziata;** and Windsor, Ontario-born lawyer and former premier of Ontario, **Ernie Eves**, now a board member of a Jamaican medical marijuana business.

- **Brian Mulroney,** who served as the 18th Prime Minister of Canada, is a mentor to British Columbia-born **Kim Campbell,** first woman Prime Minister of Canada, diplomat, lawyer and writer; and French Canadian lawyer, diplomat and former Premier of Quebec **Lucien Bouchard.**

- Truro, Nova Scotia-born former Premier of Nova Scotia and Harvard Law School graduate **Robert Stanfield** (1914-2003) is a mentor to High River, Alberta-born statesman, journalist and 16th Prime Minister of Canada, **Joe Clark.**

- Manitoba-born, award-winning businessman and U.N. official **Maurice Strong** (1929-2015) was a mentor to Ontario-born lawyer, author and businessman **Paul Martin, Jr.,** the 21st Prime Minister of Canada.

- Award-winning Canadian lawyer, women's rights and justice advocate and the person who coined the term "environmental crisis" **Michelle Swenarchuk** (1948-2008) was mentored by Quebec labour activist, aboriginal rights activist and feminist **Madeleine Parent** (1918-2012), Canadian labour union executive and author **Doris Anderson** (1921-2007), and German-born Canadian research physicist **Ursula Franklin** (1921-2016).

- Manitoba-born politician and business consultant **Gildas Molgat** (1927-2001) was a mentor to Manitoba-born Member of Parliament and Senator **Ron Duhamel** (1938-2002).

- Ontario-born 14th Prime Minister of Canada, soldier and author **Lester Bowles Pearson** (1897-1972) is a mentor to British-born Canadian lawyer **John Napier Turner,** the 17th Prime Minister of Canada.

- Manitoba-born author and philanthropist **Norah Willis Michener** (1902-1987), wife of former Governor General of Canada, is a mentor to Vancouver, British Columbia-born author, actress, photographer and social advocate for people with bipolar disorder, **Margaret Trudeau,** mother of **Justin Trudeau,** the 23rd Prime Minister of Canada.

- Montreal, Quebec-born former Speaker of the Canadian Senate **Pierre Claude Nolin** (1950-2015) is a mentor to Sudbury, Ontario-born lawyer **David Johnston,** the 28th Governor General of Canada.

- Kenora, Ontario-born politician and soldier **Alvin Hamilton** (1912-2004), who served as the Minister of Agriculture where he pioneered wheat sales to China and **Daniel Johnson,** Quebec politician are mentors to Quebec-born lawyer, businessman and 18th Prime Minister of Canada **Brian Mulroney.**

- Edmonton, Alberta-born **Mike Harcourt,** the 30th Premier of British Columbia and the former mayor of Vancouver, is a mentor to Duncan, British Columbia-born former broadcaster and politician **Moe Sihota.**

- Toronto, Ontario-born professional hockey player **Art Smith** (1906-1962) was a mentor to Calgary, Alberta-born journalist, Canadian politician and 12th Premier of Alberta **Ralph Klein** (1942-2013), who had the nickname, "King Ralph".

- Canadian grade 8 teacher **Bob McGill** was a mentor to Canadian superhero, athlete, humanitarian and cancer research activist **Terry Fox** (1958-1981).

- Former Canadian teacher and federal public servant **Kay Stanley** is a mentor to Nepean, Ontario-born politician, **John "Rusty" Baird,** former Canadian Minister of Foreign Affairs.

- Toronto, Ontario-born **Mike Harris,** former school board trustee, politician, 22nd Premier of Ontario and creator of the "Common Sense Revolution" was a mentor to Ottawa, Ontario-born **Jim Flaherty** (1949-2014), politician and federal Minister of Finance.

- Canadian former Ontario cabinet minister and former federal Minister of Finance **Jim Flaherty** (1949-2014) is a mentor to Canadian Conservative leadership candidate **Kellie Leitch.**

- **Ralph Klein** (1942-2013), former Premier of Alberta, is a mentor to Ontario-born **Stockwell Day,** politician and former leader of Canadian Alliance party.

- Canadian politician and federal cabinet minister **Wilf Spooner** (1910-2001) is a mentor to Scotland-born Canadian former member of the Ontario Legislative Assembly **Alan Pope.**

- Canadian economist and politician who was the 26th Premier of Quebec, **Jacques Parizeau** (1930-2015) is a mentor to Quebec lawyer, teacher and politician who served as the 28th Premier of Quebec **Bernard Landry** and Canadian politician **Daniel Paillé.**

- Vernon, British Columbia-born former Canadian Member of Parliament and the first person of First Nations status to serve in the federal cabinet **Len Marchand** (1933-2016) is a mentor to British-born Canadian politician **Terry Lake.**

- Former Premier of Quebec, **Lucien Bouchard,** is a mentor to Canadian politician, accountant and co-founder and CEO of Air Transat, **Francois Legault.**

- Dominican **Father Thomas Philippe,** head of Eau Vive (a centre for theological and spiritual formation for lay people), is a mentor to Swiss-born award-winning Canadian philosopher, theologian, author, humanitarian and founder of L'Arche community **Jean Vanier** (1928-), Canadian care-giver extraordinaire. Mr. Vanier said "Life is a succession of crises and moments when we have to rediscover who we are and what we really want."

- Canadian Green Party candidate in British Columbia and high school teacher **Mark Neufeld** considers **Mary Owor** his mentor.

- Canadian Green Party member, British Columbia political leader and scientist **Andrew Weaver** considers Canadian scientist **Lawrence Mysak** (physical oceanography), **Jason Middleton,** and **Ed Sarachik** (atmospheric sciences) his mentors.

- Montreal-born **Jack Layton** (1950-2011), the late leader of the New Democratic Party in Canada, was mentored by Ontario-born former leader of the federal New Democratic Party **Ed Broadbent;** and is a mentor to Nebraska-born Canadian **Randall Garrison,** federal Member of Parliament from British Columbia; Canadian **Todd Minerson** of White Ribbon; and Ontario-born nurse, educator and social justice advocate **Cathy Crowe;** as well as many other Canadians.

- Jamaican-born British Columbia politician, university professor and Order of Canada recipient **Rosemary Brown** (1930-2003) was a "mentor for virtually every woman who went into politics in the last 30 odd years," according to former British Columbia NDP leader and Minister **Joy McPhail.**

- Canadian **Mike Harris** (the 22nd Premier of Ontario) was a mentor to Canadian **Jim Flaherty,** (1949-2014), former Ontario cabinet minister and former federal Minister of Finance.

- The 10th Premier of Saskatchewan **Allan Blakeney** (1925-2011) and Canadian social democratic politician, Baptist minister and architect of Canada's healthcare system **Tommy Douglas** (1904-1986), rated the greatest Canadian of all-time, are mentors to Saskatoon-born former (12th) Premier of Saskatchewan **Roy Romanow.**

- Canadian pastor and politician **J.S. Woodworth** (1874-1942), founder of the Canadian Co-operative Commonwealth Federation, was a mentor to Canadian politician and minister **Tommy Douglas** (1904-1986), the father of universal health care and often considered the most revered Canadian of the 20th century.

- Prince Edward Island-born scientist, bomber pilot, farmer and politician **Angus MacLean** (1914-2000), Premier of Prince Edward Island, is a mentor to Saskatchewan-born farmer, businessperson, diplomat, Ambassador to Ireland and 30th Premier of PEI **Pat Binns.**

- Canadian journalist and politician **Dalton Camp** (1920-2002) was a mentor to **Norman Atkins** (1934-2010), Canadian politician and businessman.

- Hamilton, Ontario-born politician **John Munro** (1931-2003) is a mentor to Hamilton, Ontario-born former politician and Deputy Prime Minister of Canada **Sheila Copps,** who succeeded John Munro to office.

- Saskatoon, Saskatchewan-born **Roy Romanow,** the 12th Premier of Saskatchewan and the Chancellor of the University of Saskatchewan is a mentor to Winnipeg, Manitoba-born diplomat and politician **Gary Doer,** the former Premier of Manitoba and Canada's Ambassador to the United States.

- The 14th Premier of Alberta and lawyer **<u>Alison Redford</u>**, born in British Columbia, called Calgary-born **<u>Peter Lougheed</u>** (1928-2012), former Alberta premier and lawyer, her mentor.

- Winnipeg, Manitoba-born businessman, local politician and squash player **Roy Parkhill** (1931-2002) is a mentor to civil engineer and former (19th) Premier of Manitoba **Gary Filmon.**

- Ontario-born Canadian politician and 7th Premier of Alberta **Bill Aberhart** (1878-1943) was a mentor to Saskatchewan-born Canadian politician, recipient of the Companion of the Order of Canada, member of Canada's Senate and the 8th Premier of Alberta, **Ernest Manning** (1908-1996).

- Often called "Mentor to the world" because of his view of Canada's accomplishments in democratic federalism and ethnic pluralism, Canadian Prime Minister **Pierre Elliott Trudeau** (1919-2000) was considered a mentor to many politicians around the world. The Pierre Trudeau Foundation screens and selects candidates every year to act as mentors.

- **Adrienne Louise Clarkson,** a Hong-Kong-born Canadian journalist, politician, stateswoman and recipient of the Order of Canada who served as the 26th Governor General of Canada, considers **Northrop Frye** as one of her mentors. She recalled her mentor, who she met as an undergraduate at the University of Toronto: "My thoughts have developed a great deal in the 40 years, since I took his Anatomy of Criticism course. But they set me on a path thinking about our country, thinking about my own approach to literature and what it can "teach" us. I believe very much in the dream and the way in which ancestors dream their progeny into being. I have said often that immigrants particularly dream their children into a new kind of life. I don't think I would have had these thoughts, had I not worked with Northrop Frye and begun to understand what the imagination can actually do for you."

- San Francisco-born Canadian social justice advocate and front-line activist **Frances Wasserlein** (1946-2015), was a mentor to many social activists.

- **Michaëlle Jean,** Haitian-born Canadian stateswoman, journalist and the 27th Governor General of Canada launched The Mentorship Program of the Order of Canada in 2008 to bring members of the Order of Canada, women and men from all disciplines recognized for their merit and outstanding contribution, to mentor young Canadians aged 18-25 years in their fields of interest and serve as role models and a source of inspiration.

- Ontario-born **Jim Prentice** (1956-2016), who was elected as the 16th Premier of Alberta and elected to the Parliament of Canada, was a mentor to Alberta politician and Alberta government cabinet minister **Manmeet Bhullar** (1980-2105). Both men died as the result of crashes.

- Burnaby, British Columbia-born Canadian politician, leader of the British Columbia liberal party and 35th Premier of British Columbia, **Christy Clark** calls **John Nuraney** (1937-2016), the first Muslim to be elected to the British Columbia provincial legislature, her mentor.

- Canadian mandala artist, spiritual counsellor, educator, and social service advocate **Madeleine Shields** (1933-2005) was a mentor to many including **Paul Harris.**

- Canadian labour leader and social justice activist **John Shields** (1938-2017) was a mentor to many including award-winning British Columbia-born environmental activist and writer **Briony Penn** and Canadian social activist, artist, and entrepreneur **Donna Morton**, who said of her mentor, "John was my spiritual Father - it is that simple. We could literally talk about anything (and did). Sometimes, when he asked me about unhealthy patterns in my romantic life, he would pull a 'Dr. Phil' and ask in that knowing way, "How's that working for you?" I asked him why he mentored me and others right up until the end. He said it was all about potential. When he saw people with potential struggling, he could not let go. Human potential gave him a sense of life and enthusiasm that was irresistible. How could he not do this for the countless people over the course of his life?"

- Manitoba-raised Canadian women's rights advocate, feminist, labour leader, teacher and named Woman of Distinction by the YWCA, **Kay Sigurjonsson** (1933-2016) was a mentor to many women involved in politics, labour, and education.

- Canadian **Annie McClung,** a temperance and women's suffrage advocate was a mentor to Ontario-born Canadian feminist, politician, author and women's rights and social activist **Nellie McClung** (1873-1951), who became one of "The Valiant Five" that launched the "Persons Case," that contended women could be "qualified persons" eligible to sit in the Canadian Senate. The Supreme Court of Canada ruled that the current law did not recognize women as such. However, the case was won upon appeal to the Judicial Committee of the British Privy Council—the court of last resort for Canada at that time. Annie would become Nellie's mother-in-law.

- Award-winning politician, the first woman elected mayor of Saint John, an elected member of New Brunswick parliament and businessperson, **Elsie Wayne** (1932-2016) was described by **Rona Ambrose,** head of the Conservative Party of Canada, as "a strong mentor for women in politics."

- Raoul Wallenberg Centennial Medal winner for his efforts to advance human rights, former Member of Parliament and Minister of Justice, Montreal-born **Irwin Cotler** was described by Green Party of Canada leader, environmental activist, author and lawyer **Elizabeth May** as "being a mentor to others rather than using his skills to 'cut opponents to ribbons'; and is a mentor to Liberal Party of Canada leader and Canada's 23rd Prime Minister **Justin Trudeau** and NDP Member of Parliament **Murray Rankin**.

- Saskatchewan-born environmentalist **Jim MacNeill** (1928-2016), the author of the first Canadian book on environmental management, was described as an "early warrior against climate change", and was an advisor to Canada's 15th Prime Minister **Pierre Elliott Trudeau** (1919-2000), as well as a mentor to Green Party of Canada leader and elected Member of Parliament from British Columbia, **Elizabeth May**.

- British Columbia politicians **Carole James,** current NDP member of the British Columbia legislative assembly, former NDP Premier (30th) of British Columbia, **Mike Harcourt** and former NDP Premier (32nd) **Dan Miller** are all mentors to New Democratic Party leader and MLA **John Horgan** who, during the 2017 campaign, promised to introduce a new, province-wide mentoring program in concert with the RCMP to help curb gang violence.

- **Justin Trudeau,** Canada's 23rd Prime Minister considers **Mawlana Hazar Imam** (The Aga Khan), the recipient of the 2016 Adrienne Clarkson Prize for Global Citizenship, one of his mentors.

"People who don't take risks, or who don't take any steps forward, you don't hear much about them."

~ Grace McCarthy (1927-2017) ~
Vancouver-born British Columbia politician and cabinet minister
Recipient of the Officer of the Order of Canada
Started the first toll-free help line for children
Mentored by W.A.C. Bennett

Mentors Involved with Painting, Sculpture, Ceramics and Photography

- Canadian wildlife artist **Glen Loates** is a mentor to Ontario-born, award-winning artist **Janice Tanton,** who mentors a number of Canadian artists and youth in Canmore, Alberta.

- French writer, poet and founder of Surrealism **André Breton** (1896-1966), and Canadian painter Quebec City-born Canadian painter and illustrator **Alfred Pellan** (1906-1988), were mentors to Montreal-born Canadian surrealist artist and engraver **Mimi Parent** (1924-2005).

- Canadian artist and filmmaker **Jack Chambers** (1931-1978) was a mentor to Canadian realist artist **Brian Rendel Jones** (1950-2008).

- British-born Canadian ceramist, potter, scholar, garden designer and teacher **Robin Potter** (1939-2017) was awarded the Order of Canada and was considered a mentor to many young artists.

- Born in Ontario, Canadian painter, teacher, war artist, and modernist painter of self-portraits **Pegi Nichol MacLeod** (1904-1949) was mentored by Quebec-born Canadian ethnographer, folklorist and founder of Canadian anthropology **Marius Barbeau** (1883-1969), who was awarded the Order of Canada.

- British-born Canadian painter, artist, teacher and poet **Jack Shadbolt** (1909-1998) was a mentor to Canadian teacher, writer, printmaker, illustrator and painter **Molly Lamb Bobak** (1922-2014), who was the first female war artist and illustrator; and British Columbia-born Canadian muralist, painter, and upholsterer **Kazumi Kawaguchi** (1915-2010).

- Canadian Indigenous master carver, artist, hereditary chief and spirit guide, **Beau Dick** (1955-2017) was described as a "magnet and mentor; a virtuoso storyteller but also a master listener."

- Award-winning Hamilton, Ontario-born Canadian portrait sculptor, medal designer and liturgical artist **Elizabeth Bradford Holbrook** (1913-2009), co-founder of the Canadian Portrait Academy and the Canadian Group of Art Medalists and appointed an Officer of the Order of Canada is a mentor to award-winning Ontario-born Canadian portrait artist, sculptor and painter **Christian Cardell Corbet.**

- British-born Canadian painter and educator **Arthur Lismer** (1885-1969), one of the founders of the Group of Seven, was a mentor to Ontario-born visual artist and philanthropist **Isabel McLaughlin** (1903-2002).

- Award-winning Canadian portrait photographer **Yousuf Karsh** (1908-2002), called one of the greatest portrait photographers of the 20th century by *Time* magazine, and the photographer who captured Winston Churchill's angry and belligerent attitude in a classic portrait, was a mentor to American jazz icon photographer **Herman Leonard** (1923-2010).

- Canadian artist and member of the Group of Seven **Lawren Harris** (1885-1970) was a mentor to award-winning Victoria, British Columbia-born Canadian artist and writer who was inspired by the Indigenous people of the Pacific Northwest, **Emily Carr** (1871-1945); and Ontario-born Canadian painter **Tom Thomson** (1877-1917), also a member of the Group of Seven, who mysteriously died of drowning during a canoe trip on Canoe Lake in Algonquin Park.

- English landscape painter and illustrator **Stanley Royle** (1888-1961) was a mentor to iconic Toronto-born Canadian painter **Alex Colville** (1920-2013) who is a mentor to award-winning St. John's, Newfoundland-born Canadian painter and printmaker **Christopher Pratt.** Alex Colville told this story, "My school counsellor met with me and said after a battery of tests, 'you're very talented academically.' I said that's not news to me. Then he said, 'Painting is just a matter of manual dexterity.' I thought this guy is just stupid."

- Award-winning Victoria, British Columbia-born Canadian artist and writer who was inspired by the Indigenous people of the Pacific Northwest, **Emily Carr** (1871-1945) was a mentor to British Columbia-born portrait artist and recipient of the Order of Canada, **Myfanwy Spencer Pavelic** (1916-2007).

- Quebec-born, award-winning painter **Paul-Émile Borduas** (1905-1960), whose painting, *Froissement Multicolore,* sold for $663,750 at a 2012 auction, surpassing the artist's previous auction price record by $150,000, was a mentor to French Canadian sculptor and painter **Charles Daudelin** (1920-2001).

- Saskatchewan-based Canadian Cree artist **Allen Sapp** (1928-2016) was mentored by Prince Albert, Saskatchewan-born Saskatoon painter and teacher **Wynona Mulcaster** (1915-2016).

- Canadian art dealer and gallery owner **Mira Godard** (1928-2010) is a mentor to **Gisella Giacalone,** who has been the director of the Godard Gallery since 2003. "I learned everything about life, business and human nature directly from Mira, including loyalty," Ms. Giacalone said in a recent interview; "her voice will be in my mind for the rest of my days."

- Victoria, British Columbia-born **Bill Reid** (1920-1998) was a Canadian artist who specialized in indigenous art, especially Haida jewelry, sculpture, screen-printing and paintings was a mentor to Haida Gwaii Hereditary Chief and Master Carver **Jim Hunt.** "Bill taught me how to survive in the city. He helped me make sure I didn't get lost. I learned that if I wanted to work on my own stuff, I had to stay away because his energy was so great."

- Canadian archaeologist, cultural anthropologist and museum curator **Wilson Duff** (1925-1976) is a mentor to British Columbia-born Canadian First Nations artist, mural painter, carver, and sculptor, and a member of the Order of Canada, **Roy Henry Vickers.**

- Quebec-born **Paul-Émile Borduas** (1905-1960), an abstract painter, was a mentor to internationally-known, Montreal, Quebec-born painter, sculptor and Companion of the Order of Canada, **Jean-Paul Riopelle** (1923-2002), who in turn is a mentor to Montreal-born, award-winning artist **Michel Vermeulen.**

"No one ever asked Picasso whether he was influenced by Canadian art, and yet look at his masks: Who's to say Picasso hadn't seen any of our work."

~ Daphne Odjig (1919-2016) ~
Canadian First Nations artist
Awarded the Order of Canada
Mentored by her grandfather and mentor to Jerry P. White

Mentors Involved with Writing, Poetry and Print Journalism

- Austrian-born Canadian journalist, author, newspaper and magazine editor, and Companion of the Order of Canada **Peter C. Newman,** is a mentor to Canadian **Robert Lewis,** formerly Vice President of Content Development at Rogers Media and former Board Chair of the Canadian Journalism Foundation.

- Ontario-born Canadian author, editor, playwright and professor **Robertson Davies** (1913-1995) was a mentor to Kingston, Ontario-born Canadian journalist and author, **Jean Portugal** (1921-2016).

- Ontario-born Award-winning Canadian novelist **Richard B. Wright** (1937-2017) mentored many students and received the Order of Canada for his literature, poetry and mentoring.

- British-born **Tyrone Guthrie** (1900-1971), a writer and artistic director of the Shakespearean Festival in Stratford, Ontario was a mentor to Canadian author, novelist, playwright, journalist, professor and editor **<u>Robertson Davies</u>** (1913-1995).

- Born on the Six Nations Reserve in Grand River, Canadian writer, poet, artist and performer **<u>Pauline Johnson</u>** (1861-1913) said she was mentored by her grandfather, **Smoke Johnson.** She was also known as Tekahionwake or "double wampum."

- Canadian poet and writer **Pauline Johnson** (1861-1913), sometimes referred to as the "Mohawk Mentor" is a mentor to Canadian singer/songwriter, visual artist, advocate for Aboriginal rights, and award-winning mentor **Buffy Sainte-Marie.**

- Barbados-born Canadian novelist, essayist and short-story writer **Austin Clarke** (1934-2016) is a mentor to award-winning Canadian novelist **<u>David Chariandy</u>.**

- American playwright, novelist and three-time Pulitzer Prize winner **Thornton Wilder** (1897-1975), the author of *The Bridge of San Luis Rey*, was a mentor to American novelist **John Knowles** (1926-2001), the author of *A Separate Peace*, among others; and Canadian novelist and playwright **<u>Timothy Findley</u>** (1930-2002), whose work included *Famous Last Words*.

- American writer and pioneering feminist **Tillie Olsen** (1912-2007), the author of *Tell Me a Riddle*, is a mentor to Ottawa-born Canadian author and poet **Margaret Atwood** and was a mentor to American short-story writer **Grace Paley** (1922-2007).

- Award-winning Canadian writer **Bonnie Burnard** (1945-2017) served as a mentor to participants in the Humber School for Writers Summer Workshop.

- Canadian poet and academic **George Johnston** (1913-2004), Canadian literary critic and poet **Northrop Frye** (1912-1991) and English poet and novelist **Robert Graves** (1895-1985) were mentors to Canadian poet and scholar **Jay Macpherson** (1931-2012) who, in turn, served as a mentor to Ottawa, Ontario-born Canadian author, literary critic and environmental activist **Margaret Atwood.**

- Award-winning Edmonton, Alberta-born Canadian novelist, short story writer and Officer of the Order of Canada **W.P. Kinsella** (1935-2016) and author of *Shoeless Joe*, is a mentor to Canadian author **Dorothy Speak** author of *Object of Your Love.*

- American thriller fiction novelist **Tom Clancy** (1947-2013) was a mentor to Canadian author **Robert Wiersema.** Mr. Wiersema said of his mentor, "Beliefs-wise, Clancy and I could not be more distant. His lean to the far right was roughly equivalent to mine to the far left....I didn't agree with Clancy on a lot of things, but heroism transcends all politics. And story, of course, trumps all. Thank you for reminding me of that Mr. Clancy."

- Ontario-born, award-winning Canadian free verse poet, writer, editor and recipient of the Order of Canada, **Al Purdy** (1918-2000), who served in the Royal Canadian Air Force during WWII, is a mentor to Toronto-born, award-winning Canadian writer, artist and poet **Joe Rosenblatt,** who dropped out of high school in order to work in a variety of blue-collar jobs.

- Award-winning Quebec poet, teacher and editor **Endre Farkas**, who fled to Canada after the failed Hungarian uprising of 1956 to become a leading member of the English-speaking literary community in Quebec, was a mentor to Quebec-born Canadian poet, teacher and editor **Ruth Taylor** (1961-2006). She was an active member of the Montreal literary network and her last book was *Comet Wine.*

- Russian-British social and political theorist, philosopher and historian **Sir Isaiah Berlin** (1909-1997), who once said, "Only barbarians are not curious about where they come from, how they came to be where they are, where they appear to be going, whether they wish to go there, and if so, why, and if not, why not", is a mentor to Toronto-born Canadian author, academic and former politician **Michael Ignatieff,** who wrote, among other works, _The Warrior's Honor: Ethnic War and the Modern Conscience._

- Canadian journalist and author **Isabel LeBourdais** (1909-2003), the author of _The Trial of Steven Truscott_, was a mentor to Ontario-born Canadian writer, journalist, recipient of the Order of Canada, member of the Canadian News Hall of Fame, and social activist **June Callwood** (1924-2007), who wrote, among other works, _The Man Who Lost Himself: The Terry Evanshen Story._

- Saskatchewan-born Metis academic, political leader and writer **Howard Adams** (1921-2001) is a mentor to Saskatchewan-born Canadian writer, recipient of the Order of Canada, playwright, and Metis historian **Maria Campbell,** who was the producer of the Aboriginal TV series, _My Partner, My People._

- Newfoundland-born award-winning Canadian poet **E.J. Pratt** (1882-1964), called "the foremost Canadian poet of the first half of the century", was a mentor to Quebec-born Canadian literary critic and theorist **Northrop Frye** (1912-1991), whose first book, _Fearful Symmetry,_ unlocked the poetry of William Blake and brought Mr. Frye into prominence. Mr. Frye's anti-Vietnam War activism and activism to end apartheid in South Africa brought him under the scrutiny of the Royal Canadian Mounted Police.

- Yukon-born award-winning Canadian journalist, author and storyteller **Pierre Berton** (1920-2004), author of many books including _The Klondike Fever_, recalled his mentors as his Boy Scout troop leaders, and Canadian newspaper and magazine editors **Hal Straight, Jack Scott, Ralph Allen, Arthur Irwin** and **Bruce Hutchinson.**

- Edmonton, Alberta-born Canadian professor, philosopher and intellectual **Marshall McLuhan** (1911-1980) was a mentor to culture writer New York-born **Neil Postman** (1931-2003), the author of _Building a Bridge to the 18th Century: How the Past Can Improve Our Future_; and Canadian poet and York University professor **Frank Zingrone** (1933-2009), the author of _The Media Symplex: At the Edge of Meaning in the Age of Chaos_.

- American poet and short story writer **Delmore Schwartz** (1913-1966) was a mentor to Quebec-born Canadian-American author, professor and multiple award-winning writer including the Nobel Prize, **Saul Bellow** (1915-2005), and Brooklyn-born American musician, singer, songwriter, record producer and photographer **Lou Reed** (1942-2013).

- Quebec-born **Saul Bellow** (1915-2005), winner of the Nobel Prize for Literature and author of *Ravelstein*, is a mentor to U.K.-born writer **Martin Amis,** author of *Experience: A Memoir*. Mr. Amis described his mentor as "the greatest American author ever, in my view."

- American author, publisher, businesswoman and editor **Helen Gurley Brown** (1922-2012) and the editor of *Cosmopolitan* magazine for 32 years, is a mentor to Toronto-born Canadian media executive, author and former editor of Cosmo, Glamour, and Us magazines, **Bonnie Fuller.**

- Award-winning Canadian novelist and academic, born in Nova Scotia, **Hugh MacLennan** is a mentor to Toronto-born Canadian writer **Anne Coleman,** author of *I'll Tell You a Secret: A Memory of Seven Summers.*

- **Ezra Pound** (1885-1972), an American poet and critic was a mentor to Montreal-born recipient of the Order of Canada, poet, and publisher **Louis Dudek** (1918-2001); and American-born, Harvard graduate, poet, bon vivant and founder of New Directions publishing, **James Laughlin** (1914-1997).

- American literary critic **Edmund Wilson** (1985-1972), author of *O Canada: An American's Notes on Canadian Culture,* is a mentor to award-winning, Quebec City-born writer, novelist, poet and playwright **Marie-Claire Blais.**

- Canadian novelist and playwright **Timothy Findley** (1930-2002) considered British actor **Sir Alec Guinness** (1914-2000) as his mentor; and is a mentor to Canadian writers **Marie Woodrow** and **Elizabeth Ruth.**

- **Robert Weaver,** producer of literary programming at CBC radio and known as the "Godfather of Canadian Literature," is a mentor to Ontario-born **Alice Munro,** multiple award-winning Canadian writer and Nobel Prize Laureate.

- Prize-winning Canadian poet, teacher, and author of *Borrowed Beauty,* **Maxine Tynes** (1949-2011) is a mentor to dozens of Canadian women and other poets.

- **Carol Shields** (1935-2003), Pulitizer-prize author, novelist and poet was considered a generous mentor to emerging writers and was mentored by Award-winning Canadian novelist, short-story writer **Blanche Howard** (1923-2014).

- Canadian writer **Robert Kroetsch** (1927-2011) is a mentor to Canadian writer, critic, editor and university professor **Aritha van Herk** and Canadian short-story writer, **Russell Brown.**

- Romanian-born Canadian poet **Irving Layton** (1912-2006) was mentor to Canadian free verse poet **Al Purdy** (1918-2000) and hundreds of other poets.

- Romanian-born Canadian poet, known for his "tell it like it is" style, **Irving Layton** (1912-2006), Canadian poet and lawyer **F.R. Scott** (1899-1985), Canadian poet, journalist and lawyer **A.M. Klein** (1909-1972), and Spanish poet and dramatist **Federico García Lorca** (1898-1936) were all mentors to Canadian singer-songwriter, poet, visionary **Leonard Cohen** (1934-2016). Señor Lorca taught Leonard Cohen "that poetry can be pure and profound, and at the same time popular."

- American-born, award-winning Canadian novelist **Leon Rooke** is a mentor to award-winning Hamilton, Ontario-born Canadian short-story writer **Rebecca Rosenblum**.

- British Columbia resident and award-winning Canadian author of thriller novels and a *NYTimes* bestseller, *Still Missing,* **Chevy Stevens** started out using self-help books for would-be writers to initiate her career as a novelist, but she found she needed a mentor to get the help she needed. She selected **Renni Browne,** the author of *Self-Editing for Fiction Writers*, and Ms. Browne provided the university education she needed, particularly a "blizzard" of feedback and connected her to a network of others.

- Award-winning Manitoba-born Canadian novelist and short story writer **Margaret Laurence** (1926-1987), founder of the Writers' Trust of Canada, author of *The Stone Angel,* among others, and Companion of the Order of Canada, was a mentor and inspiration to many younger writers and was mentored by South African-born Canadian short story writer and novelist **Ethel Wilson** (1888-1980), who Ms. Laurence describes as one of the people who most helped and influenced her as a writer.

> **"I guess I write to trick reality into revealing itself."**
>
> ~ George Bowering ~
> Award-winning Canadian novelist, poet and historian
> Known as a mentor to generations of young writers.

Mentors Involved with Broadcasting and Journalism

- British-born, award-winning Canadian broadcaster **John Martin** (1947-2006), the creator of music television in Canada is a mentor to British-born, Canadian arts and pop culture broadcaster and writer **Daniel Richler.**

- Canadian radio broadcaster **Jack Cullen** (1922-2002), radio broadcaster **Al Jordan** (1928-2009) and Vancouver, British Columbia radio broadcaster and member of the British Columbia Entertainment Hall of Fame **Vic Waters** (1918-2008) are all mentors to Canadian broadcasting icon, pioneering rock radio disc jockey and advertising executive **Red Robinson.**

- Jamaican-born CBC broadcaster and radio announcer **Dwight Whylie** (1936-2002) is a mentor to award-winning Canadian CBC producer **Jean Carter.**

- Award-winning Australian journalist **Jack Marks** was a mentor to Canadian-born media mogul and billionaire **Ken Thomson** (1923-2006).

- Canadian journalist, editor and novelist **Ralph Allen** (1913-1966) was a mentor to Canadian broadcaster, writer and reporter **Peter Gzowski** (1934-2002), known as "Captain Canada".

- Canadian sports journalist **Milt Dunnel** (1905-2008) is a mentor to British sports broadcaster and journalist **Jim Proudfoot.**

- Canadian senator and former award-winning television journalist **Pamela Wallin** considers her sister **Bonnie George** as her mentor.

- Canadian broadcaster **Russ Froese** is a mentor to award-winning Canadian news anchor Global-TV **Suzette Meyers.**

- *Globe and Mail* Canadian editor **Greg O'Neill** (1954-2016) was a mentor to Globe and Mail editor **Stan Stanleigh,** who said Greg "mentored countless young editors, many of whom still work in the industry, all of whom would credit him for launching their careers. He would have eaten a journalism-school instructor for breakfast."

- Canadian award-winning radio host and humorist **Stuart McLean** (1948-2017) was mentored by Canadian journalist and journalism professor **Don Obe** (1929-2012), and Canadian broadcaster, writer and reporter **Peter Gzowski** (1934-2002), whom he considered a colleague as well as a mentor.

- British-born Canadian journalist **Bob Gibbens** (1924-2016) was a mentor to many Montreal journalists, including Quebec-based **Kevin Dougherty,** who has written for many Canadian newspapers.

- Canadian broadcast journalist, author, news anchor and Member of the Order of Canada, **Knowlton Nash** (1927-2014), born in Toronto, is a mentor to award-winning U.K.-born Canadian broadcaster, TV-news anchor and Officer of the Order of Canada **Peter Mansbridge.**

- Award-winning Stratford, Ontario-born Canadian TV journalist, broadcaster, news anchor and Officer of the Order of Canada **Lloyd Robertson**, is a mentor to Ontario-born Canadian TV broadcaster and journalist **Lisa LaFlamme**, and veteran TV news executive **Wendy Freeman**.

- Canadian journalist, editor, and champion of the underdog **Charles Bury** (1946-2014) was a mentor to many other journalists. One of those he mentored said, "Charlie instilled in us the importance of treating people with respect, of telling their stories fairly, accurately and with balance. It wasn't about journalism, at least not exclusively. Charlie was trying to teach us about how to live our lives, define our value systems and be good citizens."

- British-born Canadian **Ralph Hancox** (1929-2017), former CEO of *Reader's Digest Canada*, journalist, editorial writer and RAF pilot, was a mentor to many budding journalists at the Canadian Centre for Studies in Publishing.

- CBC broadcaster & radio announcer **Dwight Whylie** (1936-2002) is a mentor to award-winning CBC producer **Jean Carter**.

"A sense of morality, a passion for freedom, and a large and fearless capacity for righteous anger are at the heart of journalism. Otherwise, it's nothing but selling ads."

~ Peter Desbarats (1933-2014) ~
Canadian author, playwright and journalist
Awarded the Officer of the Order of Canada

Mentors Involved in Acting, Comedy, Performing, Theatre Arts, Producing, Directing, Magic, Cinematography, Motion Pictures and Television

- **Mark Starowicz,** a British-born Canadian journalist and producer for CBC radio and an Officer of the Order of Canada, and American television executive **Brandon Tartikoff** are both mentors to Toronto-born Canadian media executive producer and philanthropist **Ivan Fecan.**

- Edmonton-born Canadian Métis filmmaker **Gil Cardinal** (1950-2015) was a mentor to many. His legacy fund aids emerging filmmakers.

- Award-winning Canadian film director, producer, actor and founder of the Canadian Film Centre, **Norman Jewison** is a mentor to American film and television producer and director **Lee Daniels**.

- Scottish-born Canadian documentary filmmaker **John Grierson** (1898-1972) was a mentor to **Michael Spencer** (1919-2016), a Canadian film advocate, champion, director and producer.

- Edmonton, Alberta-born Canadian comedy legend, writer, musician and pot activist **Tommy Chong** (1938-2017) is a mentor to Australian journalist, television producer and comic **Wayne Darwen**.

- High school and elementary drama teacher, author, formerly the executive director of the Sears Ontario Drama Festival and drama consultant, **Wayne Fairhead** is a mentor to award-winning Canadian theatre critic, journalist, arts broadcaster, and board member of the Canadian Theatre Critics Association, **Mira Friedlander.**

- American comedian, actor, and violinist **Jack Benny** (1894-1974) was a mentor to Winnipeg, Manitoba-born Canadian singer, violinist, and comic actress **Gisele McKenzie** (1927-2003).

- American stage magician, author and television performer **Harry Blacksone** (1885-1965) is a mentor to Canadian-American retired stage magician and skeptic **James Randi.**

- Victoria, British Columbia-based Canadian stage performer, close-up magician, and magic store entrepreneur **<u>Tony Eng</u>** (1946-2008) was a mentor to generations of magicians. Mr. Eng's father did not like the tricks and slight-of-hand activities that his son would perform while working in his father's restaurant. His dad said to him, "Why don't you read some books and become a lawyer? At worst, you can be a cook." At 14, Mr. Eng found his own mentor in a barber who also performed as a magician.

- North Vancouver, British Columbia-born Chief of the Tsleil-Waututh Nation and award-winning actor **Chief Dan George** (1899-1981) was a mentor to Canadian Aboriginal award-winning actor **Gordon Tootoosis** (1941-2011).

- American comedian, actor and musician **John Belushi** (1949-1982) was a mentor to Brantford, Ontario-born comic actor, screenwriter and graphic artist **Phil Hartman** (1948-1998), who was a mentor to American comic actor and author **Julia Sweeney,** and Scarborough, Ontario-born actor, comedian, screenwriter and film producer **Mike Myers.**

- Canadian comedian, actor, and political satire pioneer, **Dave Broadfoot** (1925-2016), born in North Vancouver, British Columbia and best known for his performances on the Royal Canadian Air Farce, was mentored by Canadian actor, professor and playwright **Mavor Moore** (1919-2006).

- Multiple award-winning Canadian comedian **Jo-Anna Downey** (1967-2017) was a mentor to many other female comedians.

- Canadian inventor, film producer and co-founder of Cineplex **Nat Taylor** (1905-2004) is a mentor to award-winning Canadian film, theatrical producer and lawyer **Garth Drabinsky,** who was convicted and sentenced to prison for fraud and forgery.

- Canadian lawyer and communications executive **Andre Bureau** is a mentor to Canadian film and television executive **Lisa de Wilde.**

- Canadian actor, painter, photographer **Leonard Nimoy** (1932-2015) is a mentor to Canadian actress **Kim Cattrall.**

- Canadian Mohawk actor and athlete **Jay Silverheels** (1912-1980) is a mentor to Yaqui Native American actor, jeweler and ledger painter **Micheal Horse.**

- **Kim Collier** (Canadian theatre director and winner of the 2010 Siminovitch Prize) is a mentor to Canadian theatre director **Anita Rochon.**

- **Elizabeth Sterling Haynes** (1897-1957), drama and education visionary, was a mentor to **Leona Paterson** (1912-2004), a pioneer in speech arts, actress, and Canadian professor.

- Canadian dramaturge **Iris Turcott** (1954-2016) was a mentor to many playwrights and artistic director **Nina Lee Aquino,** who said, "She dramaturged my leadership. She was the guide that I needed to find my voice and my place...."

- Award-winning Canadian performer, director, playwright and educator **Joy Coghill** (1926-2017) was mentored by **Dorothy Somerset** (1900-1991), founder of the University of British Columbia's theatre department and **Charlotte Chorpenning** (1873-1955), children's theatre playwright, and was a mentor to many others in the theatre industry.

- TV producer **Herbert Brodkin** (1912-1990) is a mentor to Canadian actor **William Shatner.** When an optimist is asked to think of a Canadian actor, they typically reply: "Christopher Plummer." When a pessimist is asked the same question, they typically reply: "William Shatner."

- Award-winning Canadian actor **Len Cariou** played Alexander Graham Bell in the Canadian TV series, *Mentors* (1998-2005), produced and written in Canada by Canadian **Josh Miller.**

- British TV producer and director **David Walker** is a mentor to **Ian Morrison,** spokesperson of Friends of Canadian Broadcasting and former Executive Director of the Canadian Association for Adult Education.

- Canadian filmmaker, Order of Canada recipient and co-inventor of IMAX **Graeme Ferguson** is a mentor to Canadian writer, editor, producer and director **Toni Myers.**

- Canadian filmmaker **George Kackender** (1933-2016) is a mentor to Budapest, Hungary-born Canadian television and movie producer, member of the Order of Canada and member of the Canadian Film and Television Hall of Fame, **Robert Lantos**. "His film launched my career," said Mr. Lantos of his mentor. "My early filmmaking lessons were all from him. I really did not know how a film was made. I went through that process organically with him and he was the master. I was the novice."

- Canadian screenwriter, author and filmmaker **<u>Guy Maddin</u>** is a mentor to Canadian filmmaker **<u>Noam Gonick</u>**.

- Award-winning Canadian filmmaker, actor, author and member of the Order of Canada, **David Cronenberg,** born in Toronto, is a mentor to Cario, Egypt-born Canadian award-winning stage and film director, screenwriter, producer and Companion of the Order of Canada, **Atom Egoyan.**

- **Frank Loesser** (composer of broadway shows such as *Guys and Dolls* and *How to Succeed in Business Without Really Trying,* is a mentor to **Stanley (Stan) Edwin Daniels** the Canadian screenwriter who wrote TV-shows such as *The Mary Tyler Moore Show* and *Taxi,* among others.

- **William Leonard Hunt** (1838-1929), known as "The Great Farini" who was a Canadian high wire walker, botanist, painter, and inventor of the parachute was a mentor to trapeze artist **Lulu** (Sam Wasgate) (1855-1939).

- Canadian magician **<u>Dai Vernon</u>** (1894-1992), known as "the professor" because of his substantial influence in the magic world, was a mentor to Canadian magician, illusionist and politician **<u>Doug Henning</u>** (1947-2000) and American close-up magician **Michael Ammar,** recognized worldwide as one of the greatest living magicians.

- Comedian **Chris Rock** has had several mentors. He says, "I had a lot of good mentors such as **Eddie Murphy** and Canadian **Lorne Michaels.** Half of what they said wasn't about being a comedian. It was like, 'This is what you are going to have to do, and these are the tough decisions you are going to have to make, and here's the way of going about things.'"

- Quebec-born Canadian animator, voice actor and producer **John Kricfalusi,** known as "K" and the creator of the *Rin & Stimpy Show,* is a mentor to Canadian cartoonist **<u>Amir Avni</u>**. Their mentorship started through letters and Mr. Anvi said of his mentor, "What made an impact on me was that he thought I was worth it. It gave me this approval from this artist that I admire—showed me that I could take this (animation) seriously." His mentor became his mentor, he said, "because I recognized some of myself when I was a kid. I saw his dedication. He was so hard core and eager about it."

- Born in Iceland, award-winning Canadian film director and producer **<u>Sturla Gunnarsson</u>** is a mentor to Canadian filmmaker **David McCallum,** who said that he asked Sturla to be his mentor because he knew he would give him an honest opinion and not let me take the easy way out. As a result of the mentorship, David learned to let the process evolve or unfold and not be dictatorial about it.

- Award-winning French film director and writer **Eric Rohmer** (1920-2010) is a mentor to Canadian writer **Russell Smith**. Mr. Smith learned from Mr. Rohmer's films that is was possible to have an entire film and plot based on everyday dramas. "This realization made me understand that I had the experience and imagination necessary to make up similar stories. And I started writing them."

- Canadian actor, songwriter and game and talk show host **Alan Thick**e (1947-2016) is remembered as a mentor by American actress and director **Joanna Kerns** and his brother, **Todd Thicke.**

- **<u>Gary Goldberg</u>** (1944-2013), American writer and television and film producer, is a mentor to Edmonton-born Canadian American actor, author, producer and activist **<u>Michael J. Fox,</u>** who said of his mentor, "He touched so many with his enormous talent and generous spirit. He changed my life profoundly."

- New Orleans-born American crime fiction writer **Elmore Leonard** (1925-2013) is a mentor to award-winning Etobicoke, Ontario-born Canadian screenwriter, television producer and director, and actor **Graham Yost,** who is responsible for such shows as *Justified* and the *Americans.*

"All actors are defectors. They leave reality, go into fantasy. They leave who they are and become somebody else. And that's part of the business."

~ Graham Greene ~
Award-winning Canadian First Nations stage, screen and TV actor
Mentor to Lt. Dunbar (Kevin Costner) in *Dances with Wolves* (1990)
Mentor to Ed Chigliak (Darren Burrows) in *Northern Exposure*

Mentors Involved in Business, Education, Industry, Medicine, Architecture, Law, Metaphysics and Science

- Award-winning, Cobble Hill, British Columbia-born Canadian hero, pharmacologist and physician **Frances Oldham Kelsey** (1914-2015) overcame exceptional pressure from corporate interests and government disinterest and prevented thalidomide from being marketed in the USA, thus preventing thousands more children from being born with missing limbs. She was named a Virtual Mentor for the American Medical Association, and she was named to the Order of Canada.

- Toronto-born Canadian physician **Sheela Basrur** (1956-2008) was Toronto's Chief Medical Officer. When she witnessed the arrival of the deadly severe acute respiratory syndrome (SARS) outbreak, she immediately moved into problem-solving mode. She worked three weeks straight after the first cases were discovered. She led the team that charted the SARS course, trying to build firewalls between the infected and those who were vulnerable to its path. Health workers were dying along with SARS patients.

As reported in the *Globe and Mail*, "a female co-worker remembers bumping into Dr. Basrur one day during the crisis as she emerged from a washroom. The co-worker told Dr. Basrur that she looked wonderful and the doctor responded by saying she felt tired. The co-worker said, 'Sheela, you're great. The whole city loves you and is counting on you. And this morning on the radio I heard the host of the morning show say that he knew it was okay to go out because the little doctor with the glasses said it was.' Dr. Basrur laughed and hugged the woman in delight and went off to try and save more lives. Several years later, the co-worker e-mailed Dr. Basrur and asked if she remembered the incident. She said 'yes, but I believe he said cute little famous doctor with the glasses.'"

Colleagues described Dr. Basrur as a mentor for clear communication. One public health official said Dr. Basrur's gender, height, skin colour, and articulateness acted as a catalyst for her own choice of public health as a career. One of those Dr. Basrur mentored formulated a reason to pay the mentoring forward: "In memory of Dr.Basrur, I will make time to speak to young Canadians about their career choices, especially those who may identify with me ethnically or otherwise. I can't pretend to have all the answers, but if I can help someone to ask the right questions, as Dr. Basrur did for me, that may be enough."

- Edmonton, Alberta-born Canadian activist, bookseller and author of *The Canadian Encyclopedia* **<u>Mel Hurtig</u>** (1932-2016) is a mentor to Toronto-born Canadian author and activist **<u>Maude Barlow</u>**, the National Chairperson of the Council of Canadians and the recipient of 14 honourary degrees.

- Canadian businesswoman **Linda Hasenfratz**, President and CEO of Linamar Corporation is mentored by her Hungarian-born Canadian father and billionaire businessman **Frank Hasenfratz.**

- Munich, Germany-born Canadian social activist, scholar, professor and Holocaust survivor, **Dr. Ursula Franklin** (1921-2016) was a mentor to many including Canadian physician, writer and humanitarian activist **Dr. James Orbinski,** former president of Medecins San Frontieres; and Canadian senior constitutional lawyer and advocate of civil liberties and human rights **Mary Eberts,** co-founder of Women's Legal Education Action Fund (LEAF) who said about her mentor, "...She led us into a place where she trusted that we would also be able to consider things from a deeply moral standpoint. For me, it pushed me to try to think more as she would, rather than just in terms of accomplishing certain reachable objectives. It stretched me very much to have her as a mentor. And it stretched me in directions that I have perhaps been inclined to go but never really gone."

- High school and elementary drama teacher, author, formerly the executive director of the Sears Ontario Drama Festival and drama consultant, **Wayne Fairhead** is a mentor to award-winning Canadian theatre critic, journalist, arts broadcaster, and board member of the Canadian Theatre Critics Association, **Mira Friedlander.**

- Vancouver, British Columbia-born Canadian academic, science broadcaster and environmental activist **David Suzuki** acts as a mentor to the David Suzuki Foundation senior staff and Fellows. Dr. Suzuki has said that "education has failed in a very serious way to convey the most important lesson science can teach: skepticism."

- Canadian-Hungarian economist **Karl Polanyi** (1886-1964) was a mentor to Canadian philosopher, nationalist, and economist **Abe Rotstein** (1929-2015).

- Former Canadian Labour Congress (CLC) president and staunch defender of human rights and social justice **Bob White** (1936-2017) is a mentor to current CLC president **Hassan Yussuff.**

- Canadian technology entrepreneur and former CEO **Gerri Sinclair** is a mentor to **Aoife Dowling,** manager of digital strategy at a Vancouver-based credit union. Mr. Sincliar says, "My first thought when I think about mentorship is my own mentors and how I would love to apply what I've learned from them and the way they treated me."

- Founder and chair of the Forum for Women Entrepreneurs Canadian **Christina Anthony** is a mentor to **Lisa Niemetscheck,** general manager, Canadian Forum for Women Entrepreneurs.

- Canadian entrepreneur **Erin Athene** is a mentor to **Jason Guille,** Canadian producer.

- Bogota, Colombia-born **Ana Dominguez,** president of Campbell Company of Canada, provides mentoring to a number of people to help them carve their own path. She describes her role as teaching her mentees to see their passions through enough life cycles to not only apply the learnings, but to grow from the resulting self-awareness.

- Canadian YWCA CEO **Janet Austin** is a mentor to **Fiona Douglas-Crampton,** business executive.

- Canadian computer science professor **Yvonne Coady** is a mentor to software developer **Rebecca Dunn-Krahn.**

- Canadian executive banker **Nancy McKinstry** is a mentor to **Shelly Appleton-Benko,** Canadian financial adviser.

- Canadian financial business partner **Michelle Osry** is a mentor **Moses Richu,** business analyst.

- Canadian liquor executive **Barbara Philip** is a mentor to **Michaela Morris,** journalist and educator.

- Canadian business executive **Elizabeth Watson** is a mentor to **Teresa Budd,** lawyer and consultant.

- Canadian business founder **Carla Wood** is a mentor to **Stephanie Ratcliff,** account director.

- Canadian arts centre director **Donna Spencer** has been a mentor to many actors and producers.

- Canadian **Laurel Douglas,** the head of the Women's Enterprise Centre and responsible for matching thousands of entrepreneurs with women mentors is also a mentor to **Tammy Moore,** the CEO of the ALS Society of Canada.

- Canadian entrepreneur **Judy Brooks** is a mentor to **Val Litwan,** CEO of the British Columbia Chamber of Commerce.

- Canadian mechanical engineering professor **Elizabeth Croft** is a mentor to Canadian university electrical and computer engineering professor **Dana Kulic.**

- Financial investor **Bonnie Foley-Wong** is a mentor to Canadian **Jennifer Li,** co-founder and CEO of MuseFind in Vancouver, BC.

- Canadian lawyer **Anne Giardini** is a mentor to corporate executive **Wendy King**.

- Canadian professor of information systems **Rebecca Grant** is a mentor to **Jordyn Hrenyk,** producer, Animikii, Inc in Victoria, British Columbia.

- Canadian hospital executive **Barbara Grantham** is a mentor to **Teija Beck,** Canadian hospital executive.

- Digital strategist **Shauna Harper** is a mentor to Canadian media executive **Camille MacDonald.**

- Canadian law firm partner **Elizabeth Harrison** is a mentor to **Denise Nawata,** law firm partner.

- Canadian medical school professor **Maria Issa** is a mentor to Society of Canadian Women in Science and Technology president **Christin Wiedemann.**

- Canadian chief inclusiveness officer **Fiona MacFarlane** is a mentor to **Louisa Lun,** senior manager, EY, Vancouver.

- Canadian university director of entrepreneurship **Sarah Lubik** is a mentor to **Lauren Watkins,** marketing manager.
- Canadian business executive **Lois Nahirney** is a mentor to **Stephanie Bruckner,** market research manager.

- Canadian co-founder, president and CEO of a domain service **Cybele Negris** is a mentor to **Shannon Cole,** telecommunications manager.

- Detroit, Michigan-born Canadian **Ruth Bell** (1919-2015), women's rights and volunteer advocate, Order of Canada recipient, and university professor was honoured for mentoring by Carleton University. One of the people she mentored said of her, "She believed that creating dialogue requires us to suspend our own opinions when we are listening to others, and we have to persuade men and women to look beyond a person's physical appearance to discover his or her essence."

- Hamilton, Ontario-born Canadian lawyer and human rights activist, **Alan Borovoy** (1932-2015) is a mentor to many including:
    Toronto-born, award-winning human rights consultant **Karen Mock**
    Canadian former CEO of the Canadian Jewish Congress **Bernie Farber**
    American litigator & legal and political commentator **Danielle McLaughlin.**

- British-born Canadian entrepreneur, businessman and founder of Corel software, **Michael Cowpland** is a mentor to Canadian computer scientist and former CEO of Corel **Derek Burney Jr.**

- **Lloyd Dennis** (1924-2012), Canadian educator, school principal and author of *Living and Learning: The Report of the Provincial Committee on Aims and Objectives of Education in the Schools of Ontario* also known as the "Hall-Dennis Report" is a mentor to **Heather Birchall,** a Canadian school principal. Ms. Birchall said of her mentor: "I wish I could have told him the impact (inspiring me to have the courage of my convictions) he had on me in my formative years."

- British neuroscientist **Patrick Wall** (1925-2001) was a mentor to Canadian Dr. **Bruce Pomeranz** (1938-2013), a physician and and physiologist, who discovered endorphins in his research on acupuncture and was known throughout North America as the "Father of Alternative Medicine."

- **Dr. Bruce Pomeranz** (1938-2013), a Canadian physician and physiologist is a mentor to Canadian neuroscientist **Dr. Jason Lazarou.**

- Canadian plasma physicist **Tudor Johnston** (1932-2016) is a mentor to Canadian scientist **Federico Rosei,** the recipient of the 2017 Outstanding Engineer Award from the Institute of Electrical and Electronics Engineers Canada and the author, along with his mentor, of *Survival Skills for Scientists.*

- Canadian computer scientist, university professor, visionary, recipient of the Order of Canada, and part of the first team to build computers in Canada, **Calvin "Kelly" Gotlieb** (1921-2016), is a mentor to Canadian-American computer scientist and university professor **Allan Borodin.**

- Canadian neurologist, leading stroke researcher, recipient of the Order of Canada and pioneer of the use of aspirin for stroke prevention Dr. **Henry Barnett** (1922-2016) mentored many & his research on aspirin saved many.

- Hungarian pathologist **Arthur Biedl** (1869-1933), considered a founder of modern endocrinology, was a mentor to Austrian-Canadian endocrinologist and Companion of the Order of Canada **Hans Selye** (1907-1982), a leading researcher on stress who said, "Man should not try to avoid stress any more than he would shun food, love or exercise."

- British-born **Charles Darwin** (1809-1882) was a mentor to Canadian-English evolutionary biologist **George John Romanes** (1848-1894), the creator of the terms "neo-Dawinism" and "anthropomorphism".

- American ethnobotanist, Harvard educator, and scholar regarding indigenous people's uses of plants **Richard Shultes** (1915-2001) is a mentor to Harvard graduate Canadian anthropologist, ethnobotanist, photographer and author **Wade Davis.**

- Canadian Metis **Dr. Jo-Ann Episkenew** (1952-2016), author of *Taking Back Our Spirits: Indigenous Literature, Public Policy, and Healing,* educator, and advocate for native people is a mentor to First Nations University of Canada professor **Jesse Rae Archibald-Barber.**

- Canadian businessman and previous Grand Chief of the Grand Council of the Crees, **Billy Diamond** (1949-2010), was a mentor to Canadian politician, activist and Grand Chief **Matthew Coon Come**, member of the Cree Nation.

- British mathematician **Alicia Boole Stott** (1860-1940) was a mentor to **Donald Coxeter**, British-born Canadian professor who is often described as "the man who saved geometry".

- Canadian **Gwyn Morgan,** former President and CEO of EnCana Corporation, recipient of the Order of Canada, and newspaper columnist is a mentor to Canadian **Randy Eresman,** retired CEO of EnCana Corporation.

- American-born **Robert Milton,** former CEO of Air Canada, is a mentor to Romanian-born, Canadian immigrant **Calin Rovinescu,** lawyer and President and CEO of Air Canada.

- Canadian business executive and former CEO of Canadian Tire **Wayne Sales** calls **Stuart Friend,** the manager of KMart, his mentor.

- **Phyllis Yaffe,** former chief executive of Alliance Atlantis Broadcasting and chairperson at Cineplex considers **Peter Grant,** Canadian law firm senior partner and author, her mentor.

- Canadian businesswoman **Moya Greene,** former CEO of Canada Post and currently CEO of the UK's Royal Mail considers her mentors to be: retired civil servant and former Chancellor of the University of Ottawa **Huguette Labelle,** former Canada deputy minister of labour **Mark Daniels,** and Canadian academic, Officer of the Order of Canada and civil servant who was often referred to as the "dean of deputy ministers" **Arthur Kroeger** (1932-2008).

- South African-born Canadian **Jack Cockwell,** former CEO of Brascan Ltd, Director of Brookfield Asset Management, and known as one of the richest persons in Canada, is a mentor to South African-born Canadian **Kevin Benson,** Director of TransCanada Corporation, and formerly President and CEO of the Insurance Corporation of British Columbia.

- Chairman and CEO of MacLaren McCann Canada, **Howard Breen** is a mentor to **John Farquhar,** co-founder, partner and CEO of Rain 43, and formerly President and CEO of Young & Rubicam Canada.

- German-born American architect and founder of the Bauhaus School of architecture **Walter Gropius** (1883-1969) mentor to German-born Canadian architect **Cornelia Hahn Oberlander,** member of the Order of Canada and designer of Vancouver's Robson Square and Ottawa's National Gallery of Canada, among others.

- American award-winning architect, writer and educator **Frank Lloyd Wright** (1867-1959) was a mentor to Canadian architect <u>**Francis Conroy Sullivan**</u> (1882-1929); and Canadian gold medal award architect **Arthur Erickson** (1924-2009), who designed the Simon Fraser University campus in British Columbia, the Canadian Embassy in Washington, DC, among others.

- Canadian Gold Medal architect and urban planner **Arthur Erickson** (1924-2009) was a mentor to Canadian architect and urban designer **Bing Thom** (1940-2016).

- American-Canadian architect **C.E. Pratt** (1911-1996) was a mentor to Canadian architect **Ron Thom** (1923-1986), designer of Massey College in Toronto.

- German-American architect **Ludwig Mies van der Rohe** (1886-1969) was a mentor to <u>**Philip Johnson**</u> (1906-2005), known as the "dean of American architects"; and Canadian architect, philanthropist and recipient of the Order of Canada **Phyllis Lambert,** the founder of the <u>Canadian Centre for Architecture</u>.

- Ontario-born Canadian super lawyer **Edward Greenspan** (1944-2104), known as Canada's top criminal attorney, was a mentor to Egypt-born Canadian criminal attorney <u>**Marie Henein.**</u>

- Canadian energy executive **Michael A. Grandin** is a mentor to Canadian energy corporation executive **Sherri Brillon.**

- Canadian nurse educator, health care leader, nursing administrator and founder of the Ontario Provincial Nurse Administrators' Interest Group, <u>**Dorothy Wylie**</u> (1929-2016), was a mentor to many in nursing, including **Susan Smith** and **Gail Donner,** former dean of the University of Toronto Faculty of Nursing.

- British-born Canadian sociology professor, psychoanalyst, an early director of the Canadian Mental Health Association, and political activist **John Seeley** (1913-2007) was a mentor to Toronto-born Canadian criminal justice lawyer and Member of the Order of Canada, **Clayton Ruby;** and Toronto-born Canadian novelist, playwright, journalist and critic **<u>Rick Salutin</u>.** Mr. Ruby said of his mentor, "He was more important in my life than either of my parents. Mr. Salutin said of his mentor, "He picked up everything I was concerned about before I'd finished the sentence and replied, as always, with astute sensitive advice." Professor Seeley's son said when his father was ill and passing, "you could feel all of what he had distributed around the world coming back to him in letters, visits and phone calls, and so many of them said the same thing: that he had touched their lives in a way that nobody else had and that he was like a father to them."

- Vancouver, British Columbia-born Canadian computer scientist and philanthropist, former University of British Columbia undergraduate, University of Waterloo graduate student and currently a a professor at Stanford University, **David Cheriton** is a mentor to the founders of Google and has donated more than $27 million to Canadian universities to benefit thousands of science students.

- Canadian philanthropist, athlete, mentor and thoracic surgeon, **Bill Nelems** (1939-2017), who participated in the world's first lung transplant and the use of a blood test to detect changes related to lung cancer, established <u>The Okanagan-Zambia Health Initiative</u> to bring Canadian medical professionals to Zambia to act as mentors to their Zambian peers and improve the quality of medical care.

- Canadian-born **Maurice Strong** (1929-2015) is a mentor to Hungary-born, Canadian businessperson, philanthropist, Founder and Chairman Emeritus of Barrick Gold Corporation **<u>Peter Munk,</u>** who, in turn, is a mentor to business executives **Jamie Sokalsky** and **Randall Oliphant,** and helped establish the cardiac mentor program at the Peter Munk Cardiac Centre.

- Alberta businessperson, founder of Atco Ltd and the founder of Spruce Meadows equestrian centre, **Ron Southern** (1930-2016) is called a mentor by his daughter Alberta-born **Nancy Southern,** award-winning business executive. She said of her father, "He didn't always agree with me; we weren't always the best of friends. But he always had my back, and I always had his. I don't think I would have ever been ready for the job had he not started preparing me when we lived back at the trailer factory site when we first started. I will be forever thankful to him for that. I feel lonely without him, but I don't feel lost."

- Canada's CFO of the year for 2017 business executive **Michael Rousseau** indicated his mentors included Norm Latowsky, CEO of United Cigar Stores, who taught him professionalism, good listening skills and the role of business leadership; business executive **Robert MacLellan** who taught him the importance of focus, being direct and decision-oriented; and business executive **Calin Rovinescu,** who helped him learn about passion, strategic intensity, flexibility and courage.

- American physicist **Joseph Henry** (1797-1878), the first secretary of the Smithsonian Institution, an inventor of the first telegraph, and a pioneer in weather observation which led to the creation of the U.S.Weather Bureau, was a mentor to Scotland-born Canadian, American inventor, scientist, and engineer, credited with producing the first practical telephone **Alexander Graham Bell** (1847-1922), who learned the Mohawk language and was awarded the title Honorary Chief.

- **John Porter** (1921-1979), known as Canada's most distinguished sociologist of his time, mentored whole generations of sociologists, particularly those enrolled at Carleton University where he taught for 30 years. He pioneered the view that contradicted the popular opinion at the time that Canada was a democratic "classless society" in his award-winning book and controversial book, The Vertical Mosaic (1965). Instead, Dr. Porter emphasized the relationship between class structure and power.

- Saskatoon-born Canadian businessperson, billionaire entrepreneur and philanthropist **Jimmy Pattison** is a mentor to former radio announcer and retired Chairman of the Jimmy Pattison Broadcast Group (JPBG), **Rick Arnish**.

- Historian and award-winning author **Michael Bliss**, professor of history at the University of Toronto, recipient of the Order of Canada and member of the Canadian Medical Hall of Fame is a mentor to McGill University history professor and author **Elspeth Heaman.**

- An early advocate of preventive medicine, Vancouver, British Columbia-born Canadian medical doctor **Roger Hayward Rogers** (1928-2011) who emphasized the importance of exercise and vegetables in the diet and was considered a revolutionary because of his interest in health rather than disease and after whom the $250,000 Dr. Rogers Prize in complementary medicine is named, is a mentor to Canadian doctor **R. Winona Rowat.**

"You can do science anywhere. Obviously, it's a tremendous challenge to do it in space."

~ Dr. Roberta Bondar ~
Sault Ste. Marie-born Canadian astronaut (Space Shuttle Discovery, 1992)
Mentored by Dr. Lloyd Sippell

Mentors Involved in Music, Songwriting and the Music Business

- Victoria, British Columbia-born Portuguese Canadian singer, songwriter and record producer **Nelly Furtado** calls Canadian singer, songwriter and music producer **Gerald Eaton** of The Philosopher Kings her mentor, according to the *Kamloops Daily News*.

- Canadian organist **Léo Le Sieur** (1897-1983) was a mentor to Montreal-born member of the Canadian Songwriters Hall of Fame **Lucille Dumont** (1919-2016), was a singer and radio and television host and known as the grande dame of chanson.

- American jazz valve trombonist **Bob Brookmeyer** (1929-2011) was a mentor to Minnesota-born multiple Grammy Award composer and bandleader **Maria Schneider;** and London, Ontario-born Canadian jazz trombonist, Canadian Boss Brass leader, composer and arranger, and Order of Canada recipient **Rob McConnell** (1935-2010). Susan Smith, writing about Mr. McConnell's death from cancer in the *Globe and Mail,* said, "Because jazz owned his soul, it kept him up nights jamming in bars around town and sent him in search of mentors."

- Canadian songwriter and singer **Kurt Swinghammer** is a mentor to Canadian singer and songwriter **Rex Sexsmith**.

- **Ustad Shahid Parvez**, known as the "world's best sitar player," is a mentor to Canadian sitar player and co-founder of the Sitar School of Toronto, **Anwar Khurshid.**

- Russian-born, American violinist **Jascha Heifetz** (1901-1987), considered the greatest violinist of all-time, is a mentor to Oxford, England-born Canadian violinist and Victoria, British Columbia cosmetic surgeon **Mark Lupin** and Indonesia--born pianist and violinist **Ayke Agus.**

- Canadian jazz pianist, bandleader, composer and arranger **Gil Evans** (1912-1988), born in Toronto, is widely recognized as one of the greatest orchestrators in jazz, playing an important role in the development of cool jazz, and modal jazz, and is a mentor to Minnesota-born composer and big band leader **Maria Schneider**.

- Born in Hoboken, New Jersey, singer, actor and producer **Frank Sinatra** (1915-1998), one of the best-selling singers of all-time, is a mentor to Winnipeg-born, Vancouver-based singer <u>**Kenny Colman**</u>.

- American singer/songwriter performer **Prince** (1958-2016) was a mentor to Canadian singer/songwriter, and dancer **Denise Matthews** (1959-2016), also known as "Vanity."

- Professor Emeritus of Flute and former Director of the Hampton School of Music at the University of Idaho, and currently at the Lionel Hampton School of Music in Anacortes, Washington, **Richard Hahn,** is a mentor to Victoria-based multi-talented Canadian musician **Tom White.**

- California-born, award-winning West-Coast Canadian musician and singer/songwriter **Shari Ulrich** is described as a mentor to many Canadian songwriters.

- Canadian agent for musicians and CEO of The Live Tour Artists company, **Doug Kirby,** who died in 2009 is a mentor to Canadian folk musician. singer and songwriter <u>**Valdy,**</u> who has been an influence and a mentor to many folk and roots artists in Canada.

- American folk blues singer **Josh White, Sr.** (1914-1969) and Canadian writer **George Ryga** (1932-1987) are mentors to South African-born, award-winning South African-born Canadian singer/actress/spiritual teacher <u>**Ann Mortifee**</u>.

- Edmonton, Alberta-born Canadian rock band performer who played with Chilliwack, the Hometown Band and Skylark and co-wrote the lyrics for the gold record song *Wildflower,* <u>**Doug Edwards**</u> (1946-2016), is a mentor to Victoria, British Columbia-born Canadian-American record producer **David Foster.**

- Canadian vocal coach, pianist, radio broadcaster and recipient of the Order of Canada **Stuart Hamilton** (1929-2016) was described as a "great mentor and a great friend to everybody."

- Canadian musician **Al Pease,** who played for 27 years with the Royal Canadian Air Force Band and also played for years at Butchart Gardens in Victoria, is a mentor to many other Canadian musicians including guitarist and bandleader **Avram McCagherty.**

- New Westminster, British Columbia-born Canadian radio host, actor, and DJ **Terry David Mulligan** is a mentor to Dawson Creek, British Columbia-born Canadian folk music singer/songwriter **Roy Forbes.**

- Toronto-born Canadian jazz vocalist and pianist **Carol Welsman** is mentored by father and sax player **George Welsman** (1920-2008), award-winning Canadian music publisher **Tony Tobias,** and French soprano **Christiane Legrand** (1930-2011).

- American guitarist and music educator **Lenny Breau** (1941-1984) is mentor to Winnipeg, Manitoba-born Canadian musician and songwriter **Randy Bachman.**

- Winnipeg, Manitoba-born Canadian musician, songwriter and founder of The Guess Who and Bachman-Turner Overdrive, **Randy Bachman** is a mentor to Winnipeg, Manitoba-born Canadian musician, singer, and songwriter **Burton Cummings** and Vancouver-born, award-winning music manager **Bruce Allen.**

- Victoria, British Columbia-born Canadian blues musician, creator of the Victoria (BC) Blues Bash, annual music event, and non-profit executive **John Fisher** (1947-2017) was a mentor to multiple young musicians who were in his bands or his classes.

- Winnipeg, Manitoba-born Canadian musician, singer, and songwriter **Burton Cummings** is mentor to English singer, songwriter, musician **Robert Plant,** the lead singer and lyricist for Led Zeppelin.

- Montreal-born Canadian pianist and sax player **Steep Wade** (1918-1953) was a mentor to Montreal-born award-winning Canadian jazz pianist **Oscar Peterson** (1925-2007).

- Award-winning Canadian jazz pianist **Oscar Peterson** (1925-2007) is a mentor to New York City-born American jazz pianist **Benny Green**.

- Victoria, British Columbia-born Canadian musician and record producer **David Foster** is mentor to Burnaby, British Columbia-born Canadian-Italian jazz, pop, big band and easy listening singer **Michael Bublé.**

- Canadian fiddler, composer and music producer **Oliver Schroer** (1956-2008) is a mentor to many young musicians. Those he mentored said that they learned "nothing was too crazy or wrong when playing the violin." "Embrace any mistake and turn it into something cool." "He just made you want to go out and do great stuff; expand your sense of what is possible." "Learn how to live life."

- The Father of rock 'n' roll, American guitarist and singer **Bo Diddley** (1928-2008) was a mentor for many rock heroes, including Order of Canada recipient **Ronnie Hawkins;** Canadian-born leader of The Band, songwriter, film composer, producer, actor, author and Order of Canada recipient **Robbie Robertson;** the Rolling Stone's British-born guitarist **Ronnie Wood**; and The Beatles. Bo Diddley felt that his role as a mentor was never properly acknowledged. "I opened the door for a lot of people, and they just ran through and left me holding the knob," he said in an interview in 2003.

- Canadian musician, known as the Ambassador of the Saxophone, **Paul Brodie** (1934-2007) was a mentor to founding member of the National Arts Centre Orchestra **Jean-Guy Brault** and concert saxophonist and composer **Daniel Rubinoff.** Mr. Rubinoff said of his mentor that he contributed to his career as a saxophonist but also helped him learn life lessons about how to talk to an audience, how to be tough about criticism, how to cold call a concert promoter and how to set up a music studio. Mr. Brault echoed the lessons learned from his mentor: "He changed my life. He opened my eyes to so many things—the realities of the professional music world."

- Award-winning Canadian singer, songwriter **Justin Bieber** says his mentor is American award-winning singer, songwriter, dancer **Usher.** "He teaches me to stay humble through this whole process, because it can get shady, the business. You've got to be humble. You've got to be grounded."

- Montreal-born Canadian folk music singer-songwriter, member of the Canadian Songwriters Hall of Fame, Member of the Order of Canada and recipient along with her sister **Anna McGarrigle** of the Lifetime Achievement Award from SOCAN, **Kate McGarrigle** (1946-2010) was a mentor to Juno award-winning Regina, Saskatchewan-born Canadian folk singer-songwriter and Member of the Order of Canada **Connie Kaldor** and many others. Ms. Kaldor said of her mentor, "She let us know that as a woman you can keep your own vision, that you can sing of things that women know, that you can, no matter how difficult, choose how you integrate country, family and career—and write music that matters. They (with her sister Anna) opened the good doors and changed how women in this industry were perceived."

- American writer, screenwriter and speaker **<u>Neale Donald Walsch,</u>** author of *Conversations with God,* is called a spiritual mentor by Ottawa, Ontario-born Canadian-American singer/songwriter, musician, multi-instrumentalist, record producer and actor **Alanis Morissette.**

- Award-winning, Montreal-born Canadian singer, songwriter, poet, novelist, painter and member of the Canadian Music Hall of Fame **Leonard Cohen** (1934-2016) is a mentor to Montreal-born, Egyptian-Lebanese-Canadian pop and jazz singer, dancer and poet **NEeMA** (Nadine Neemeh).

- Quebec-born Canadian singing superstar and businessperson and philanthropist **Céline Dion,** who has cited many artists as having an influence on her, described her late husband Quebec-born music producer, talent manager and singer **René Angélil** (1942-2016) as her mentor. Under his mentorship, Celine Dion became one of the greatest stars in the history of pop music, earning two SOCAN Awards, 20 JUNOs, five Grammys, seven American Music Awards, and 10 Billboard Awards, among countless others.

- American-born Canadian Grammy Award winning musician, saxophonist, flautist and spiritual teacher **Paul Horn** (1930-2014), whose flute playing inside the Taj Mahal established the genre of "new age music," is a mentor to many musicians including American multi-genre flautist **Gary Stroutsos,** who plays a variety of flutes in unusual settings and specializes in Native American music; and rock and folk performer **Glen Dias.**

- Canadian poet, songwriter, Ottawa cab driver and musician, **William Hawkins** (1940-2016) is a mentor to Ottawa-born Canadian singer, songwriter and member of the Canadian Songwriters Hall of Fame, **Bruce Cockburn.** Bruce said of his mentor, "Bill was an inadvertent mentor to me. I don't think he would have seen himself that way, but he had that influence and it was important to me. We were both interested in the mystical and metaphysical things that were around in the '60s. And I had been studying the beat writers in high school and I equated Bill with the great beat poets. I held him in great esteem."

- Award-winning Edmunston, New Brunswick-born Canadian singer, actor, musician and TV-host **Roch Voisine** who wanted to be a professional hockey player but had to set aside his plans as a result of a serious injury while playing baseball, was mentored by award-winning Quebec director and producer and Officer of Canada recipient **Jean Bissonnette** (1934-2016).

- Canadian music teacher **George McRae** was a mentor to Estonia-born Canadian violinist, trombonist and music teacher **Mati Sulev** (1941-2017).

- Canadian-born artist, singer, songwriter, and musician **Joni Mitchell** was mentored by Australian-born Canadian teacher, professor, and educator **Arthur Kratzmann** (1924-2015), who was a mentor to hundreds of teachers and school administrators while he was a teacher in Saskatchewan, a university professor in Alberta and a professor at the University of Victoria in Victoria, British Columbia. While a teacher to Joni Mitchell (then known as Roberta Joan Anderson) in grade 6 in Saskatoon, Saskatchewan, he helped her find her own voice. When he first met her she said she was scared to go into grade 7 because everyone there can write. Dr. Kratzmann said to her, "Don't be scared. Anyone who can paint such beautiful pictures with a brush can do the same thing with a pen." That idea stuck with her. "She also had a tendency to paint and copy others," he said. "I told her she had to learn to 'paint in her own blood.' That also took hold of her." She dedicated her first album to her mentor.

- Gatineau, Quebec-born Canadian **Paul Demers** (1956-2015), a singer and founding president of the Association des professionels de la chanson et de la musique, is considered a mentor to generations of young Francophone artists.

- Canadian country music singer who recorded more than 140 albums, born in Halifax, Nova Scotia and member of the Canadian Music Hall of Fame, **Hank Snow** (1914-1999) was a mentor to Mississippi-born American singer songwriter, often referred to as the "King of Rock and Roll," **Elvis Presley** (1935-1977); and Ontario-born Canadian country music singer songwriter, musician and member of the Canadian Country Music Hall of Fame, **Myrna Lorrie.**

- **Dr. Dale Louis,** former Dean of the University of Manitoba Faculty of Music is a mentor to Manitoba-born, award-winning Canadian musician, composer, harpist, pianist, member of the Order of Canada, and awarded the Doctor of Laws by the University of Manitoba, **Loreena McKennitt.**

"I went through the agonies of trying to be a serious musician. In Canada, in 1938, I twigged to the fact that I'm a comedienne."

~ Anna Russell (1911-2006) ~
Singer and comedienne

Mentors Depicted in TV, Movies and Book Fiction

- Ontario-based Detective William Murdoch (played by **Yannick Bisson**) is a mentor to Constable George Crabtree (played by **Jonny Harris**) in the Canadian TV-drama series *Murdoch Mysteries,* based on the novels written by Maureen Jennings.

- Kaspar Weiss (a violin prodigy played by Austrian-Hungarian musician Christoph Koncz) is mentored by George Pussin (played by Swiss film actor Jean-Luc Bideau) in the 1998 Canadian movie, *The Red Violin,* directed by Quebec-born French-Canadian screenwriter **François Girard.**

- Napoleon (played by Canadian Saul Rubinek), Edgar Allen Poe (played by Canadian Michael Sarrazin), Joan of Arc (played by Canadian Lisa Jakub), St. Nicholas (played by Israeli-born British-Canadian Brian George), Ludwig von Beethoven (played by Canadian Henry Czerny), Harriet Tubman (played by Sarah Caldwell), Frederick Banting (played by American-Canadian Matt Frewer), Elizabeth I (played by Canadian American Margot Kidder), Sherlock Holmes (played by Canadian William B. Davis), Albert Einstein (played by American Elliott Gould), Alexander Graham Bell (played by Canadian Len Cariou), Cleopatra (played by Canadian Ellie Harvey), Daniel Boone (played by Canadian Rowdy Roddy Piper), and Oscar Wilde (played by British actor Simon MacCorkindale) were all mentors to **Dee Sampson** (played by Canadian actress Sarah Lind) and **Oliver Cates** (played by Canadian actor Chad Krowchuk) in various episodes of the Canadian TV-series, *Mentors*, Award-winning Canadian producer **Kevin Dewalt,** Executive Producer.

- **Graham Greene,** an award-winning Canadian First Nations stage, screen and TV actor, played the role of a mentor to Lieut. Dunbar (played by Kevin Costner) in *Dances with Wolves* (1990) and played the role of a mentor to Ed Chigliak (played by Darren Burrows) in the TV-series *Northern Exposure.*

"I was born in 1948. I can't recall a world before television, but I know I must have experienced one."

~ William Gibson ~
Canadian American speculative fiction writer who coined the term "cyberspace" and came to Canada to avoid the Vietnam war draft
Mentored by American novelist and short story writer John Shirley

Mentors Involved in Classical and Performing Arts

- Ukrainian-born Italian composer and conductor **Igor Markevitch** (1912-1983) is a mentor to Canadian conductor and motivational speaker **Boris Brott.**

- Canadian politician and art patron **Jean-Pierre Goyer** (1932-2011) is a mentor to **Yannick Nézet-Séquin,** conductor of Montreal's Orchestre Métropolitain.

- Canadian award-winning composer and symphony music director **Bramwell Tovey** is a mentor to Canadian multiple award-winning violinist **James Ehnes.**

- American opera soprano and specialist in Wagnerian repertoire **Jessye Norman** is a mentor to British-born Canadian opera mezzo-soprano **Susan Platts.** The mentoring relationship began in 2004 as part of the Rolex Mentor and Protege Arts Initiative.

- Hungarian singer, voice teacher and vocal consultant **Vera Rozsa** (1917-2010) is a mentor to Nelson, British Columbia born Canadian soprano **Nancy Argenta.**

- Canadian baritone **Bernard Turgeon** (1931-2016) is a mentor to Canadian soprano and member of the Hall of Fame, **Chantal Lambert** and many other singers. In describing the transformative power of her mentor Ms. Lambert said, "He would challenge the singers to bring out what was special inside themselves that no one else could give. It had immediate results. The singers were suddenly freer and blossomed in front of your eyes, just by the warmth he was transmitting."

- Award-winning Canadian director and choreographer **Brian MacDonald** (1928-2014) is a mentor to Canadian National Film Board commissioner and French-born Canadian theatrical producer **James Domville** (1933-2015), who said of his mentor, "He set me on my future course and thereby changed my life."

> *"If you can feel in a vast audience that even one person knows, understands and appreciates the study you have put upon a role to make it true to life, you are rewarded for your pains."*
>
> ~ Kathleen Howard (1884-1956) ~
> Niagara Falls, Ontario-born opera singer

Mentors Involved in Sports, Sports Coaching, Athletics and Sports Business

- Born in Ireland, Canadian public servant, author (*Wild Colonial Boy*), recipient of the Order of Canada and chief planner for the 1986 World Expo in Vancouver, **Patrick Reid** (1924-2015); and **Stan Stronge,** recipient of the Order of Canada, all-around Canadian athlete until he became paraplegic from a car accident in 1940 and the founder of the Canadian Wheelchair Sports and Recreation Association and member of the British Columbia Sports Hall of Fame; and Canadian athlete, humanitarian and cancer research activist **Terry Fox** (1958-1981), who received the Companion of the Order of Canada, are all mentors to Man-in-Motion Leader and Canadian Paralympian **Rick Hansen.**

- Canadian professional ice hockey player and scout **Garnet "Ace" Bailey** (1948-2001), who perished at the World Trade Center, is a mentor to Canadian superstar professional ice hockey player and team owner **Wayne Gretzky.** In 1988, the Edmonton Oilers traded Wayne Gretzky to the Los Angeles Kings, shocking the hockey world and, in particular, those fans who were also Canadians. The outcry was so loud that one Canadian Member of Parliament, **Nelson Riis** (currently a businessman and a mentor to Canadian politician **Bill Sundhu**), tried to get the government to step in: "I figure the federal government could purchase Gretzky's contract and then resell him to a Canadian team," he suggested, continuing by proclaiming that "the bottom line is that we have to keep Wayne in Canada, where Canadians can see their greatest hockey player ever on a regular basis."

- Former Canada National Team coach, former head coach of an NBA team, and retired NBA player **Jay Triano;** and Canadian sports rehab specialist **Alex McKechnie** are mentors to Victoria, British Columbia-born retired National Basketball Association All-Star player, businessperson and philanthropist **Steve Nash.**

- Former head coach of the Canadian national men's basketball team, recipient of the Order of Canada, member of the Canadian Basketball Hall of Fame **Ken Shields** was a mentor to Ontario-born University of Victoria basketball coach **Guy Vetrie** (1952-2003), who died suddenly while jogging at UVic.

- Hall of Fame Canadian golfer **Dan Halldorson** (1952-2015) is a mentor to Canadian tour pro **Graham DeLaet**.

- Edmonton, Alberta-born Canadian, University of Victoria graduate, world champion cyclist and member of the Mountain Bike Hall of Fame and the British Columbia Sports Hall of Fame, **Alison Sydor** says she acts as her own mentor.

- Canadian swim coach, author and member of the Alberta Sports Hall of Fame & Museum and the International Swimming Hall of Fame, **Debbie Muir** is a mentor to Calgary, Alberta-born Canadian swimmer and three-time Olympic medalist **Mark Tewksbury,** who began swimming at the age of eight.

- Canadian swimmer and three-time Olympic medalist **Mark Tewksbury** is a mentor to Vancouver, British Columbia-born Canadian three-time Olympic gold medalist rower **Marnie McBean.**

- British Columbia-born Olympic gold medalist rower and author **Marnie McBean** is a mentor to Ontario-born three-time world champion and Olympic gold medalist boxer, model and humanitarian **Mary Spencer.**

- Kingston, Ontario-born Canadian retired Olympic triathlon champion **Simon Whitfield** is a mentor to Toronto-born Canadian sprint kayaker and Olympic gold medalist **Adam van Koeverden**.

- Russian figure skating coach **Tatiana Tarasova** is a mentor to Canadian ice dancing champions Ontario-born **Shae-Lynn Bourne** and German-born **Victor Kraatz.**

- West German figure skating coach, choreographer and former skating competitor **Uschi Keszler** is a mentor to Ontario-born Olympic and Canadian figure skating champion and member of Stars on Ice, **Elvis Stojko** (named after Elvis Presley by his Hungarian parents).

- Canadian award-winning figure skating coach **Richard Gauthier** is a mentor to Canadian pairs figure skater **David Pelletier,** who is married to his co-gold medalist partner, **Jamie Salé.**

- Canadian figure skating coach and gold medal skating competitor **Anna Forder McLaughlin** is a mentor to Ontario-born former World and Canadian National figure skating champion **Barbara Underhill.**

- Ontario-born Canadian former competitive figure skater and three-time Canadian national champion **Elizabeth Manley** is a mentor to Montreal-born Canadian competitive medal-winning figure skater and six-time Canadian national champion **Joannie Rochette.**

- Barrie, Ontario-born award-winning Canadian freestyle skier, pioneer of the superpipe event and four-time Winter X Games gold medalist **Sarah Burke** (1982-2012) is a mentor to Squamish, British Columbia-born Canadian skier **Rosalind "Roz G" Groenewoud,** multiple X Games Champion.

- Coach **George Stewart** is a mentor to Toronto-born alpine skiing world champion, Olympic downhill racer, member of the Canadian Ski Hall of Fame and the Ontario Sports Hall of Fame and Officer of the Order of Canada, **Steve Podborski,** who started skiing at two years old.

- **Sensei Nakamura** is a mentor to Canadian retired Olympic and Pan American games judoka medalist and member of Judo Canada's Hall of Fame **Keith Morgan.**

- Canadian boxing champion and member of the Canadian Sports Hall of Fame **Sammy Luftspring** (1916-2000) is a mentor to **Spider Jones,** Golden Gloves champion and member of the Canadian Boxing Hall of Fame.

- French Canadian **Louis Cyr** (1863-1912), who could lift 227kg with one finger and backlift 1,967kg was a Montreal policeman who was known as the "strongest man that ever lived" and was mentored by his **grandfather.**

- Trainer **Ken Hamilton** is a mentor to Toronto-born, retired gold medal boxer and member of the Ontario Sports Hall of Fame **Shawn O' Sullivan.**

- Middleweight boxer and motivational speaker **Rueben Hurricane Carter** (1937-2014), who was wrongfully convicted of murder and later released after spending 20 years in prison, became a Canadian citizen and the executive director of the Association in Defence of the Wrongly Convicted from 1993-2005, is a mentor to Canadian lawyer and motivational speaker **Lesra Martin.**

- Jamaican-born Canadian former sprinter and Olympic medalist and track coach **Tony Sharpe** is a mentor to Scarborough, Ontario-born Canadian track champion, Olympic and Pan American games medalist **Andre De Grasse.**

- Retired Canadian world champion hurdler **Perdita Felicien,** a supporter of Count Me In, the largest youth-run organization in Canada, was mentored by **Miss Arthurs,** who talked her into coming out for track in grade four and her agent, American-born **Renaldo Nehemiah,** a former NFL player and former world record holding hurdler.

- Head coach of the Canadian national women's hockey team, most successful NCAA women's hockey coach and former player **Shannon Miller** is a mentor to the staff of the Russian women's hockey team.

- Montreal, Quebec-born NHL Hall of Fame retired hockey player **Mario Lemieux** is a mentor to NHL Czech player **Jaromir Jagr** and Halifax, Nova Scotia-born award-winning NHL superstar **Sidney Crosby,** who scored the game winning goal against the United States in overtime for Team Canada in the 2010 Winter Olympics in Vancouver.

- Quebec-born Canadian retired NHL coach and record holder for the most wins in the regular season and the Stanley Cup playoffs **Scotty Bowman** is a mentor to Ontario-born professional hockey coach **Mike Keenan.**

- Ontario-born former professional ice hockey player and member of the Hockey Hall of Fame **Bobby Orr,** often referred to as one of the greatest hockey players of all time, is a mentor to Canadian astronaut, physician, engineer, scientist **Dr. Robert Thirsk.**

- Spanish tennis great and retired former world number one player **Carlos Moya** is a mentor to Yugoslavian-born Canadian tennis champion **Milos Raonic.**

- Halifax, Nova Scotia-born Canadian equestrian team athlete and member of the Order of Canada **Ian Millar,** who holds the record for the most appearances at the Olympic games, is a mentor to Ottawa, Ontario-born World Cup equestrian and show jumping Olympic medalist **Jill Henselwood.**

- Spanish race car driver **Oriol Servià** is a mentor to Oakville, Ontario-born race car driver **James Hinchcliffe,** who competes in the IndyCar series motorsports.

- Canadian **Liz Ashton,** former president for 14 years of Camosun College in Victoria, British Columbia was a three-time Olympian on the Canadian equestrian team. She specialized in eventing, where riders compete in cross-country jumping, stadium jumping and dressage. She won the Gold Medal at the 1978 World Championships, and is a member of the Canadian Eventing Hall of Fame. Her mentor is Toronto, Ontario-born **Jim Elder** who competed in six Olympic games and won gold for Team Canada in the 1968 Olympic Games.

- Edmonton, Alberta-born Canadian bobsleigh three-time Olympic gold medalist, who originally trained as a decathlete, **Pierre Lueders** is a mentor to Hawaiian-born **Justin Kripps,** a Canadian bobsled Olympic medalist and World Cup slider, who originally trained as a relay outdoor track runner.

- Scarborough, Ontario-born Canadian & Indy professional auto racing driver **Paul Tracy** is a mentor to California-born, American professional stock car racing driver **A.J. Allmendinger.**

- Canadian trampoline coach and manufacturer of trampolines **Dave Ross,** the Canadian National Team coach, is a mentor to Toronto-born Canadian trampoline gymnast and Olympic competitor, gold medal winner at the 2003 and 2007 World Championships, and gold medal at the 2007 Pan American Games competitor **Karen Cockburn.**

- Toronto-born Canadian trampoline gymnast and Olympic competitor, gold medal winner at the 2003 and 2007 World Championships, and gold medal at the 2007 Pan American Games competitor **Karen Cockburn** is a mentor to Ontario-born Canadian gold medalist in trampoline **Rosie MacLennan.** Ms. Cockburn described their mentoring relationship: "I've learned just as much from her as she has from me. We complement each other well as teammates because although we have a lot of similarities we do have different strengths. She pushes me out of my comfort zone when I'm scared. I help her think through strategies and calm her down if her mind is racing."

- Toronto-born Canadian Olympic and World Championship gold medalist sprint kayaker **Adam van Kouverden** is a mentor to Burlington, Ontario-born Canadian sprint canoeist and Olympic and World Championships gold medalist **Mark Oldershaw.**

- Jamaica-born, retired Canadian sprinter and gold medal winner in the Olympic Games, the World Championships and the Commonwealth Games, who once held the record for the 100 metres dash and member of the Ontario Sports Hall of Fame, **Donovan Bailey,** is a mentor to Jamaican-born Canadian sprinter and Olympic Games gold medalist **Akeem Haynes.**

- Valhalla, Alberta-born six-time world former wrestling champion **Christine Nordhagen** is a mentor to Stittsville, Ontario-born Canadian Olympic, Commonwealth Games and Golden Grand Prix Ivan Yarygin gold medal wrestler, **Erica Wiebe**.

- Canadian professional hockey player **Ryan Smyth,** former captain of Canadian hockey teams in international competitions, is a mentor to **Brayden Schenn,** LA Kings hockey player and scoring leader in 2010 World Junior Hockey championships.

- Vegreville, Alberta-born **Ernie Fedoruk** (1931-2010), Canadian sportswriter and fishing columnist, is a mentor to Sarnia, Ontario-born Canadian **Alex Robertson,** former hockey player and sports broadcaster. Robertson noted that Ernie knew everything about fishing especially catching fish on Vancouver Island, his home base. "One day when Ernie took me fishing" Robertson said of his mentor, "we found ourselves out in the water with hardly anybody else around and I got kind of worried and said, 'Hey, at least there are two other people in a boat.' Ernie laughed and said: 'Hey, Robertson, those are two seagulls on a log.'" Mr. Fedoruk died in Victoria, British Columbia of Alzheimer's disease.

- Toronto Canadian three-time Olympic gold medal competitive swimmer **Penny Oleksiak** will likely become a mentor for thousands.

- Fredericton, New Brunswick-born Canadian cross-country mountain bike world champion and medalist **Catharine Pendrell** is eager to provide mentoring to others.

- Australian triathlete and Olympic gold medalist **Emma Snowsill** is a mentor to Nanaimo, British Columbia-born Canadian and Olympic triathlete, **Kirsten Sweetland.**

- American-born Canadian football player, coach, teacher and school principal and member of the Canadian Football Hall of Fame **Bernie Custis** (1928-2017) was the first black professional quarterback and a mentor to Burlington, Ontario-born Canadian Football Hall of Fame member **Tony Gabriel.**

- Retired Medicine Hat, Alberta-born Canadian hockey great **<u>Trevor Linden</u>** calls Hamilton, Ontario-born, award-winning NHL coach **Pat Quinn** (1943-2014) his mentor. "He was instrumental in shaping me as a person and as a leader. ...He taught me to be a professional both on and off he ice." A Canadian, Pat Quinn, was best known for coaching Team Canada to the gold medal for the first time in 50 years at the 2002 Olympics. He was also a mentor to Victoria, British Columbia-born Canadian former NHL player **<u>Geoff Courtnall</u>,** who said, "He helped me become a better player...He prepared you well and then let you fail or succeed."

- Canadian swim coach **Randy Bennett** (1963-2015) is a mentor to Victoria, British Columbia-born, retired Canadian Olympic medalist, Commonwealth Games champion, double gold medalist in the Pan Pacific swimming championships and world champion freestyle swimmer **Ryan Cochrane**.

- Calgary, Alberta-born championship athlete, member of the Canadian Golf Hall of Fame, and member of the Alberta Sports Hall of Fame, golfer **Betty Stanhope-Cole** (1937-2017) was a mentor to young players and the Canadian Ladies Golf Association.

- Edmonton, Alberta-born retired professional hockey player, considered one of the greatest players of all time, 15-time All-Star and member of the Hockey Hall of Fame **Mark Messier** said his father and former ice hockey player, **Doug**, is his mentor.

"I want people to be inspired that I've always strived for excellence and I've always gone beyond what anybody ever thought I could do, what I thought I myself could do. And I've allowed myself to be inspired, kept my eyes open and my senses open to inspiration around me."

~ Dr. Clara Hughes ~
Winnipeg-born Canadian cyclist and speed skater and humanitarian
Olympic medalist
Officer of the Order of Canada
Mentor to Canadian triathlete Simon Whitfield and
others through <u>Let's Talk</u> and <u>Right to Play</u> initiatives

---

References

Carr, R.A. (Winter 1999). Dancing with roles: Differences between a coach, a mentor and a therapist. *Compass: A Magazine for Peer Assistance Mentorship and Coaching, 15,* 1, 5-7. (Available as PDF download for Peer Resources Network members at: http:// www.peer.ca/Projects/compassprn1.html)

Carr, R.A. (2004). Pinpointing the differences between mentoring and coaching. *Peer Bulletin 123* (Retrieved February 22, 2012 from the Peer Resources' members only area.)

Carr, R.A. (2004). *Mentor as coach.* (Retrieved February 22, 2012 from the Peer Resources' members only area.)

Carr, R. (March 29, 2017). A true mentor is always considered in the present tense. *Medium: The Step Up.* (Retrieved May 5, 2017 from here.)

Cialdini, R. (2007). *Influence: The psychology of persuasion.* New York: Harper Business.

Garringer, M. (2011). "It may be the missing piece" - Exploring the mentoring of youth in systems of care. *Reflections from the 2011 Summer Institute on Youth Mentoring.* Portland, Oregon: Portland State University. (Retrieved February 18, 2012 from http://pdx.edu/ youth-mentoring/publications)

Gray, W.A. (2011). *Mentoring relationships that work.* (E-book published by and available through Smashwords)

Kaplan, J. (2007). Coaching versus therapy. Available directly from the author, who is a member of the Peer Resources Network by sending an email to Jeff Kaplan.

Marum, P. (April 2011). Board approves improved definition of ICF Mentor Coaching. *Coaching World.* (Retrieved February 22, 2012 from the ICF website here.)

Murray, M. (2001). *Beyond the myths and magic of mentoring: How to facilitate an effective mentoring process, revised edition.* San Francisco: Jossey-Bass.

Pelan, V. (February 17, 2012). The difference between mentoring and coaching. *Talent Management.* (Retrieved February 23, 2012 from here.)

Spinelli, E. (December 2007). *Coaching and therapy: Similarities and divergences.* Paper presented at the 3rd Annual BPS SGCP National Counselling Psychology Conference, December 18, 2007. (Retrieved February 22, 2012 from the Peer Resources' members only area.)

Zukav, G. (2010). *Spiritual partnership: The journey to authentic power.* New York: HarperOne.

Mentoring Stories

On the next seven pages there are narratives about mentoring that were obtained from interviews. The persons interviewed for the first six stories asked that their names not be revealed. Some details in the story were edited to protect their identity. The photos associated with the stories are not related to the storyteller.

The seventh story is told by the author about a relationship with one of his mentors.

Additional narrative stories about mentoring are available on the Peer Resources Mentoring website here.

A Banking Career is Curtailed for Lack of a Mentor

I was glad to leave high school. It was a drag and I never did connect with anyone. I guess I was kind of a loner. Since I was pretty good with numbers, I got a job in a local bank. Handling money was fun, but it was tough, demanding work. I had to account for every penny. I thought I had a chance to improve my career at the bank so I took part in all the training programs the bank offered and I decided to go to college at night. I also read a lot of self-help books. All of this I thought would propel me up to the bank's head office. But I noticed that the men who had come to work in the bank spent a much shorter time in their positions before they were promoted. This really bugged me because I had really performed well during the training activities and was getting good grades in my accounting and financial planning courses. I decided to work harder. My choice didn't seem to work. Now when I saw others promoted over me, I resented them and my bosses. My atittude went down the tubes. I started to take more days off; after all, what good did it do to show up for work? Eventually I was laid off. Upon reflection I wish I had learned more about the problems women face in male dominated careers. I especially wish that I could have connected with a successful professional woman who had the savvy and experience to help me not be a victim.

S.B.

©Peer Resources

Navigation Tools for the Heart, Mind, and Soul®

250-480-9698

An Accidental Mentor Saved My Life

My mom was a sweet lady, but my dad was really abusive. She seemed helpless and unable to protect me. She was just as afraid of my dad as I was. I couldn't wait to leave home. I thought if I was older I could survive better so I tried to look older. I met some pretty rough guys. They introduced my to drugs, sex and the street. They weren't mentors although they protected me some. Mostly they exploited and manipulated me. During a trip to hospital for a drug overdose, I met a nurse who wanted to know how I had gotten into living the street life. Rather than berating me and urging me to go home to my parents, she asked about what I was getting out of street life. She wanted to know how my dreams of my future were being realized by being on the street. When I left the hospital we arranged to meet again and

after that we met many times. She told me about how she had overcome a physically and sexually abusive childhood and how somebody had taken an interest in her. She encouraged me to explore other options, build on my talents, and find ways to heal the wounds inside me. With her support I got a job doing exactly what I wanted to be doing. It took some struggle and a few years, but it was worth it. I'm alive.

C.C.

©**Peer Resources**

Navigation Tools for the Heart, Mind, and Soul®

250-480-9698

A Mentor Helped a Disabled Athlete Move from Despair to Hope

Not everyone will make the same mistake I did. I skied into an area that was posted as dangerous. A week later I woke up in hospital with a permanent injury to my spinal cord. I would never be able to walk, let alone ski. I was in constant pain. As far as I was concerned my life was over. I would need a wheelchair for the rest of my life. I would forever be dependent on others; no driving my car, no job, no dating, and no sex. Who would want to be with a cripple? I know I wouldn't. I had visitors for awhile, but eventually they stopped coming. My attitude and condition was probably too much for them. I felt completely helpless, hopeless, and despondent. One day a guy with a grey beard wheeled in to see me. He crashed right into my bed and let out a cheery, "Whoops!" That was my introduction to Matt. He lost his legs in a car crash. He knew what I was thinking before I knew it myself. But he listened to my self-pity and endless complaining. And he always asked me, at the end of my diatribe, "What do you want to do about it?" Often he would share with me what he did about it—the struggles, the frustrations, the disappointments. He told me about his job in a computer warehouse, about his play-making ability on a wheels basketball team, and he told me about the intimacy and sex he had with his girlfriend. But mostly he listened and challenged me to get on with my life. I'm playing on the same basketball team now, and I even outscored him.

N.W.

An Elder Uses a Story to Mentor

During my childhood, I remember mostly that my father drank and knocked me around. He worked at different jobs, but was usually home when I got back from school. I didn't like coming home without my mom being there, but she worked full-time as a housekeeper in a motel. One day my dad got mad because I didn't want to get smokes for him. He kicked me and broke my rib. As soon as my mom got home she drove me straight to my grandfather's house. I hardly knew him, because he lived on the reservation. She told me I was going to live there for a while. I was eight years old. Ten years later I moved to a place of my own. I guess you could say my grandfather became my mentor. My parents, who were both Crow, never talked about their Indian life, but my grandfather was full of stories, legends, and songs. He taught me about traditions and customs that were part of my ancient heritage. While I knew I was one of the First People on Earth, I think my parents felt shame about it. Kids at school called me apple pie — red on the outside and soft, white mush inside. I didn't know what that meant until my grandfather, Running Wolf, explained how the whites and Crows divided up the world, and how the whites settled for prejudice, while the Crows opted for wisdom. He also taught me about healing plants, respecting the earth, and my inner life. My pain and my mother's anguish brought me to this place. I guess you can benefit from adversity.

C.R.

A Mentor Dies and His Legacy Lives On

I am saddened by the death of my friend and mentor. Our souls were intertwined from the start, but events in recent years broke our capacity to express what we meant to each other. We both longed for what we had been to each other, yet neither of us could find the path for a return.

Many others who were the glue between us, knew of the public reasons for our estrangement, but only he and I knew what really happened. Knowing the private reason or tolerating the public perception does not diminish my love for him. Nor does it reduce the impact he had on my life.

We could exchange ideas, thoughts and feelings of a personal and professional nature all in the same sentence. Our life work shared the same DNA. When we worked on projects together, we both achieved greater heights than either of us could have ascended to alone.

We yearned for the same things. We held hands, we locked arms, and we laughed uproariously when we encountered common obstacles. Once when we discovered a memo that called us "a pair of axxholes," we were more delighted than offended.

Our friendship, companionship and ability to learn from each other was probably deeper and more intimate than most men are able to attain in their lifetime. I am grateful for what we had and I will always treasure everything that we were to each other.

The smile and twinkle are gone. The greeting and enthusiasm that set aglow the inner fire are now memories. A twist of fate allowed us to have time together before death claimed his body. Our conversation brought joy to both our spirits and the healing path emerged.

Death, we both discerned long ago, turns us all into philosophers. Tragedy requires us to reassess our relationship with the temporal world and the expanse of the universe. My mentor said, "Why wait for such trauma to occur? Why not help people know themselves in the world without having to gain such knowledge through tragic circumstance?"

He called this help "socio-dynamic" counselling. With a few simple principles he launched a system that has influenced helping professionals around the world and has left a legacy of practitioners, researchers and teachers.

His death, like his life, touches our most inner world. Despite our grief, our tears and our longing for him, we carry forward the larger question that was most dear to his being: "What is my place in the cosmos?" And within that question we struggle with a more immediate enquiry: "What can I do to help?"

I cannot say what I will miss most. The suspenders? The unique clothing? The Moroccan chicken? The unwillingness to engage in chit-chat? The fine wines? The insights? The stories of ranch life? The garden oasis? The gatherings? The walks? The battles with the dragons? The challenge to engage? Doing your best? Living authentically? Inspiring writing? Emotional intelligence? Road trip snoring?

What we meant to each other, what we did for each other, and how we were to each other has left me with exceptional solace. I wish, however, that I could have said "I love you," before only his soul could hear me.

Oh, brother, where art thou? Are you yet again paving the way for my travels?

250-480-9698

INDEX OF NAMES

DISCLAIMER AND CANADA 150 LOGO COPYRIGHT

The "Canada 150" logo which appears anywhere in this document is displayed as the result of a license from the Government of Canada. The use of this logo does not mean or imply that the Government of Canada endorses or is affiliated with any product or service of Peer Resources or Rey Carr. The Government of Canada is the owner of the copyright of the Canada 150 logo and its variations. No external funding was provided to prepare, produce or distribute this document.

The design was created by Ariana Cuvin, a University of Waterloo student, who submitted her entry along with hundreds of other students from across Canada. The Canada150.gc.ca website says the design is a maple leaf, made up of four diamonds, to represent the four provinces that formed Confederation. The nine other diamonds expanding outwards were meant to represent the six other provinces and three territories. The repeated shape is meant to create a sense of unity and the 13 shapes forming the leaf represents Canadians' togetherness as a country.

Note that the term "Canada 150" does not mean that Canada is 150 years old. It is meant to signify that it has been 150 years since Canada became a Confederation. Many peoples and cultures existed in Canada prior to Confederation.

www.ingramcontent.com/pod-product-compliance
Lightning Source LLC
Chambersburg PA
CBHW080522030726
47592CB00012B/3444